The Tuppenny Punch and Judy Show

The Tuppenny Punch and Judy Show

25 Years of TV Commercials

JO GABLE

LONDON
MICHAEL JOSEPH

For my mother who bought our first television set in 1953. And Daniel and Abby – children of the video age.

The colour illustrations in this book are reproduced by kind permission of the following:
Lloyds black horse – Lloyds Bank/McCann Erickson Advertising Ltd; Dulux dog – ICI Paints Division/Foote Cone & Belding Ltd; Esso tiger – Esso/McCann Erickson Advertising Ltd; Arthur – Spillers Petfoods/Geers-Gross; Evian – Schweppes Agencies/TBWA; pilchard – Glenryck/McKay & Partners; punks – Lee Cooper/Zetland's; Philips Video – Philips/Wasey-Campbell-Ewald Ltd; Mothercare – Mothercare/Masius, Wynne-Williams & D'Arcy-Macmanus; Foster Grants – Foster Grants/The Kirkwood Company; Cinzano Rosé – Cinzano/Collett, Dickenson, Pearce & Partners.

First published in Great Britain by Michael Joseph Ltd
44 Bedford Square, London WC1
1980

ISBN 0 7181 1858 8

Filmset and printed by BAS Printers Limited,
Over Wallop, Hampshire
and bound by Dorstel Press Ltd, Harlow.

Designed by Guy Shanley

Contents

PART 1
'In a Golden Coach'
When Wireless Ruled the Waves

1953: Anne Shelton – Vera Lynn – Archie Andrews – Pharos and Marina – the Coronation of Queen Elizabeth II.

If a 'national mood' can be captured, part of the essence must lie in those trigger names and part in events that simultaneously involve an entire population. Of the names of 1953, Anne Shelton and Vera Lynn – both 'forces' sweethearts' – were firmly established in Britain's pop scene. Their careers had taken off during the war that had ended just eight years before; and they had earned that special affection given to those who have 'been through it together'.

The wooden dummy Archie Andrews, along with his ventriloquist Peter Brough, represented another side of the British spirit in 1953. Archie starred in a radio show called 'Educating Archie'. The public loved the show, which ran for nine years from 1950 with a weekly listening audience of over ten million, and accepted without question the curious contradiction between the art of ventriloquism – that the dummy should be seen to be talking while his operator's lips didn't move – and the fact that Peter Brough was performing on radio. Nevertheless, 'Educating Archie' can take credit for providing many of the great names on today's entertainment scene. In nine years of shows the list of 'guests' reads like an A to Z of British showbusiness:

Artists

Julie Andrews	Bruce Forsyth	Warren Mitchell
Bernard Bresslaw	Alexander Gauge	Ken Platt
Max Bygraves	Tony Hancock	Beryl Reid
Pearl Carr	Hattie Jacques	Harry Secombe
Ronald Chesney	James Robertson Justice	Graham Stark
Jerry Desmonde	Peter Madden	Eric Sykes
Dick Emery	Bernard Miles	The Tanner Sisters

Writers

Ronald Chesney	Marty Feldman	Eric Sykes
David Climie	Harry Gibbs	George Wadmore
Sid Colin	Bill Martin	Ronnie Woolf
Pat Dunlop		

Opposite: On 27 February 1953 the Queen and the Duke of Edinburgh saw Peter Brough and Archie Andrews in a special variety performance at Broadcasting House. Peter and Archie are chatting with Hermione Gingold.

Above: Anne Shelton

Centre: Vera Lynn being interviewed by the BBC Swedish Service.

The same unquestioning trust was afforded to another popular pair of radio entertainers – Pharos and Marina. Their billing in the *Radio Times*: 'Can you beat Pharos and Marina?' cued in the listening millions to 'The Forces Show', where the couple performed a weekly mind-reading act for the studio audience – meanwhile keeping the radio listeners in real suspense and wonderment at their telepathic achievements. Even more than a radio ventriloquist, the wholesale admiration for radio mind-readers seems to sum up that easy suspension of disbelief and relish of fantasy so necessary for people relieved of war.

Then, with the Coronation of Queen Elizabeth, came a new realism. The country, having faced and mourned a major bereavement at the death of King George VI, was awaiting a change of monarch. More importantly, the crowning of the new Queen was to be televised by the BBC, making a unique occasion accessible to a population largely distanced from the event.

People who had been until then content to watch organized 'television evenings' at their local electricity showrooms now contemplated the purchase of their own television sets (the most expensive domestic electrical

appliance to have been marketed on such a mass scale) and decided to buy.

From that moment, a country where gas was the main fuel for both lighting and cooking, where the benefits of mains radio had just about won the battle with accumulator-powered wireless (only the most stubborn or least well-off being prepared to put up with the regular inconvenience of lugging the accumulator to the radio shop for a 'top-up'), took its first steps towards an electronic, mass-communicating future – but not too quickly.

Day to day life was returning to normal, or rather better than normal. Food rationing was almost at an end in 1953 and by 1954 had finished completely. Coupons were no longer needed for any kind of purchase and goods were available in the shops to buy. And if people needed any help in choosing, there were plenty of advertisements all around, and sometimes above, to inform them.

There was even, according to an unnamed member of Cheam Chamber of Commerce, advertising on BBC television. In February 1954 he roundly condemned the BBC's practice of taking cameras into leading London stores, particularly when, in the case complained of, an assistant displayed a 75/-

article at sale time and said it had been genuinely reduced to 17/6d. The Cheam member claimed it had been fairly easy to identify the store from the TV screen and was considering 'a strongly worded protest to the BBC'.

Advertising on television? Unthinkable.

The first-ever entertainment broadcast advertised to the British public was sponsored by the *Daily Mail*. Transmitted from the Marconi works in Chelmsford on 15 June 1920, it featured Dame Nellie Melba in a recital of songs. She began with 'Home Sweet Home' and ended with the National Anthem.

Two years later the BBC (British Broadcasting *Company*), the brainchild of a group of electronic equipment manufacturers who had decided at a meeting on 18 October 1922 to promote 'wireless telephony', eventually had to seek commercial sponsorship because of financial problems. The British Broadcasting Company made its first public broadcast on 14 November 1922. After only a few months it faced a money crisis, and the government set up the Sykes Committee to report on future plans for wireless broadcasting.

The Committee recommended that, as far as finance was concerned, there should be no direct advertising (i.e. companies could not pay to advertise their own products on air) but the BBC could run sponsored programmes. The Company had already taken money from sponsors who paid for broadcast concerts in return for a mention of their name, and the Committee agreed that this source of revenue could continue.

Harrods, the *News of the World, Daily Herald, Weekly Dispatch, Daily Graphic, Answers* and *Titbits* all helped the little company along until the Crawford Committee in 1925 recommended that the British government buy out the private shareholders in the BBC. This was accepted and the British Broadcasting Corporation was created on 1 January 1927.

But television advertising? A committee headed by Lord Selsdon was set up as early as 1934 to consider how television should be run, and among its suggestions was that advertising could help towards the cost of the proposed new television service.

Fifteen years later, when the Labour Party was in power, the Beveridge Committee considered plans for television in Britain even more fully, eventually concluding that advertisers could not make use of British wavelengths. The voting of the Committee was 11 to 4 against, and the minority included the chairman himself, who 'saw no danger in permitting limited advertising'. Selwyn Lloyd, another of that minority, went further and submitted a minority report that called for an independent commercial television company. In his view, properly controlled advertising sponsorship would not degrade the service.

The 1951 General Election brought the Conservative Party back to power, and it was faced with the immediate problem of planning future broadcasting policy, since the BBC charter expired at the end of that year. The Postmaster-General, Earl De La Warr, extended this for a further six months.

It was well known that the majority of Churchill's cabinet was opposed to commercial broadcasting, and it was thought that the BBC would therefore be handed a continued monopoly. But after a meeting of the 1922 Committee in November 1951 (attended by fewer than one-third of the Conservative members) the attitude seemed to soften, and the majority feeling was that it was time to end the BBC monopoly – not necessarily in favour of commercial broadcasting.

Three newly elected Conservative MPs – John Rodgers, Charles Orr-Ewing and John Profumo – who had set up an informal broadcasting group, then began lobbying for a commercial alternative. John Rodgers, MP for Sevenoaks, had worked with J. Walter Thompson, the largest advertising agency in Britain, and had founded the British Market Research Bureau. Charles Orr-Ewing, MP for Hendon North, had worked for BBC TV making arrangements for outside broadcasts, later becoming consultant to a number of electronics firms, including A.C. Cossor. He had once said that the BBC was too slow in equipping itself with post-war apparatus. John Profumo, MP for Stratford-on-Avon, had been very impressed by the sponsored television he had seen on a visit to the United States.

The pro-commercial television lobbyists agreed that tactically it was best to keep a low profile and avoid any clash with the government. To persuade rather than impose, as it was essential to gain the Prime Minister's support. Winston Churchill did not like commercial television, the 'tuppenny Punch and Judy show' he called it, but he was not over-keen on the BBC either. The Corporation had denied him broadcasting opportunities twenty years before and also, he suspected, had helped towards his defeat in the 1945 General Election. When Churchill finally stated his view it was in favour of discontinuing the BBC monopoly.

By this time the pro-commercial lobby had gained many talented and powerful advocates, one of whom was Norman Collins – a former BBC Programme Controller and Controller of BBC Television. Collins had been the prime candidate for the newly created post of Director of Television at the BBC (a position which included a seat on the Board of Management). It was then rumoured that someone else was being favoured for the job, and Collins told the Director-General that if this were true he would offer his resignation. The rumour proved well founded and Collins immediately resigned from the BBC. Described as 'the man who

Archie did appear on television – eventually.

did more than any single individual to bring commercial television to Britain' (*The Observer*), Collins put his considerable wealth of experience and belief in the future for television into the fight for a commercial service.

In the end, he and the commercial lobby won the day in spite of opposition from what could be considered the backbone of the Conservative establishment – leading churchmen; educationalists of every kind, from University Chancellors to infant school teachers and headmasters; leading businessmen; and the powerful Lord Beaverbrook, who raged against commercial television in the columns of the *Daily Express*, which then had the highest circulation in the country.

Even a last-minute push by a hastily formed National Television Council, cleverly timed to make its first approach in the press two days after the coronation, did not succeed. The British newspapers had been full of praise for the BBC coverage and contemptuous of the way American sponsored television had covered the same event – that is, presenting advertisements during the Coronation ceremony. Pepperell's Bed Sheets were advertised during the Communion service; General Motors introduced a collection of badges called America's Crown Jewels; another car was described as a 'Queen of the Road'. That one station had the gall to include an appearance by the then world-famous chimpanzee J. Fred Muggs seemed utterly barbaric . . .

The Independent Television Act finally became law on 30 July 1954, and in August the Independent Television Authority advertised for programme contractors. By November three companies, including Norman Collins' Associated Broadcasting Development Company (which became ATV), had been given the go-ahead, and in Norman Collins' words, 'the real work started'. Remarkably, Independent Television was ready for transmission in less than a year.

PART 2

'We Got Along Without You Very Well'

Ads before ITV

Having brought advertisers to the brink of commercial television, it would be as well to consider how they managed without this new medium. Very nicely, thank you, would appear to be the case, not only for the advertisers but also for the agencies who prepared their advertising, and for the many industries that provided the agencies and the advertisers with the hardware they needed to get the message across.

Commercial radio was available on 208 metres, medium waveband, on Radio Luxembourg, the original Ovaltiney recruitment centre where time was 'H. Samuel Everite Watch' time and Orson Welles was caretaker of 'The Black Museum'. Radio Luxembourg's pulling power could be phenomenal. In 1954 one 75-word advertisement drew 229,000 replies.

The cinema was another major advertising medium. A 1954 survey showed that thrice-weekly cinema visits were quite common, and that more men went than women. The poorest off went most often; the lower middle class (where the head of the family earned between £400 and £750 yearly) went less frequently; and the middle class and well-to-do (where the family head earned more than £750 annually) went least of all. This economic division limited the kind of products that could be advertised profitably.

Newspapers and magazines could hardly lose in the years just prior to the start of Independent Television. Advertisers had to book well ahead in the most popular publications to make sure of space. In January 1954, *Vogue* magazine took a full page ad in at least one advertising trade magazine to announce that it could accept no more advertisements until March.

The then British Transport Commission went all out to attract advertisers to its sites on the Underground, outside stations and in and around buses. Potential advertisers were shown examples of three-dimensional advertising and giant sixteen-sheet poster sites. They were also presented with figures to enable them to place their advertisements in the best location. In 1954, 71% of women passengers travelled on the lower deck of Central London buses and 62% of men on the upper deck. Each Central London bus carried an average of 1,066 passengers daily, and an average 500 passengers a day used each carriage on the Underground. (Today's London buses carry an average of 621 passengers daily and around 428 people travel in each carriage of the underground.)

Bomb-blasted sites around the country were seized on as ideal locations for poster hoardings, and business boomed for the makers of showcards and outdoor stove-enamelled signs – now so keenly sought after by collectors in the plastic and chipboard eighties.

Packaging was considered for its intrinsic qualities and was designed to catch the eye of the shopper, with no thought to how it would show up on a television screen. Advertisers would vie with one another to produce the most attractive point-of-sale display that would guarantee the best spot on the shop's counter.

People could wipe their feet on advertisements or rest their drinks' glass on them. They could go to a sponsored event like the 'Pepsi Olympics' or the 'Quaker Cycle Race', or if sufficiently interested they could marvel at the fifty miles of advertisements that accompanied the Tour de France in 1954. Manufacturers could even take a gamble and launch a product slightly like a consistent brand-leader and get involved in a law suit with its accompanying publicity – like Wolsey with its launch of X-fronts underpants. Quick to protect its own letter – the unchallenged byword in pants – Lyle & Scott leapt in and saved their Y for posterity, in a case that lasted almost two weeks.

Not content with the scope and variety of media open to them, and only a matter of months before the passing of the Independent Television Act, the advertising world was approached with wild and amazing ideas that bordered on the surreal.

On one occasion in February 1954 members of the Advertising Creative Circle – not people to suffer fools gladly – were alerted by their guest speaker to the danger that they might overlook 'exciting new developments in the reproduction of the human voice because they were concentrating upon the possibilities of television'. The speaker, Lynton Fletcher, a chairman of Recorded Sound Ltd and the Association of Professional Recording Studios, recalled for the audience his pre-war success with 'Godfrey, the mechanical man', who described his own workings for the BBC radio programme 'In Town Tonight', and also 'Lumena, the transparent woman', who spoke about her own digestive functions. The use of broadcast techniques and the quiet conversational voice for exhibition purposes was, he said, only beginning to be realized. He told the meeting he had been surprised at the success of his 'publicity telephones' – one had been installed at the Advertising Creative Circle and was in constant use before the dinner began. He spoke of one of his exhibition pieces – a telephone where visitors had to dial TUM in order to hear the voice of 'Mr Tum' brightly declare that mustard aided digestion; the difficulty, the speaker admitted, was to keep the six

YOU ALWAYS SEE AN

SIGN

henever you feel like saying 'That's a good sign!'
well, the chances are that it was made by Acme.

ou always *see* an Acme sign because it is
stinctive — by every standard: design, work-
anship, colour and finish.

most all the well-known names appear sooner
later on Acme signs. Why not join them *now*?

AND SIGN COMPANY LIMITED
STREET · LONDON W 1 · Telephone: GROsvenor 7458
orks · Enfield · Middlesex · Telephone: HOWard 1651
James Watt Street · Birmingham 4 · Telephone: Central 2325   ACME

Above: *Woman's Own's* circulation climbed to nearly
3,500,000 at one point before it declined and rose again to
over two million at the end of 1979.

Left: A typical sign ad of 1954.

New look for an old corner

THIS once-derelict street corner is now a friendly and attractive meeting place. The seats are a specially popular feature. And this is a first-rate poster position. Right amongst the shops. Away from competitive displays. Doing a day-long selling job. There are Advertising Sites like this—right at the point of sale—in all commercial areas of England and Wales.

ADVERTISING SITES LTD

56/60 STRAND, LONDON, W.C.2. TELEPHONE: TRAFALGAR 4922-3-4

DIRECTORS : I. A. Allam (Managing Director) S. E. Carter P. W. Felton R. H. Lawson

MEMBERS OF THE SOLUS OUTDOOR ADVERTISING ASSOCIATION LTD.

A blitzed corner becomes a poster oasis.

When shops were smaller and dirty footprinters were noticed.

A gas of an ad for neon (1955).

Left: Neon ads at Morecambe illuminations in 1954.

Right: £4,000 cubed, and you could see his lips move.

telephones serviced because they were in constant use. He had known queues of women form behind a telephone in order to hear the voice of a popular writer deliver the briefest of advertising messages. There were, he thought, great possibilities in the field of 'advertisements over the phone', because where they had been tried the success had been marked. The attraction of hearing 'Lady Blank' describe how a face-cream had changed the entire course of her life for the better, merely by dialling an easily remembered number, seemed to him to be packed with advertising potential.

The speaker then outlined three notable future possibilities. Firstly, the use of stereophonic sound in window and/or exhibition displays. In this, the objects would describe themselves and exchange conversation with one another, and the voices would in each instance appear to have come from individual objects. Secondly, the use of an attractive mechanical model seated or standing at a store entrance to speak to passers-by about the clothes she was wearing or the gadget on a table before her, was both 'traffic stopping' and 'persuasive' as a selling medium. Thirdly, there was the kind of novel description that could be arranged for mechanical moving parts, e.g. a moving crankshaft groaning for want of a little oil . . . the oil is administered . . . and the sound changes to one of grateful thanks to 'Blank & Co's oil, which never fails to produce smooth running.'

In January 1955, what was claimed to be the biggest publicity gimmick ever conducted in the radio trade was staged when

The unsensational ad for a sensational advertising medium.

RGD Ltd (Radio Gramophone Development Company) transported a giant birthday 'cake', measuring twelve feet across, ten feet high and topped by twenty-five electric candles, from their Glasgow factory to Hastings' store in Clapham Junction – for the store's official opening by Lady Barnett. The giant pink, white and silver 'cake' was given a champagne send-off from Glasgow, with Jimmy Logan cracking a bottle and fifty children singing 'Happy Birthday to You'. Mobile police escorted the four-ton truck with its curious load through many of the large towns and cities en route. Display ads were taken in all the provincial papers along the way, and local dealers were supplied with stickers listing the districts through which the cake would be passing; in several areas the lorry parked outside RGD dealers for photographs to be taken.

This confectionery caravanserai was accompanied by a film crew who were filming the event for future showing at trade exhibitions, and the culmination of the Cyclopean 'Operation Cakewalk', as the organizers fondly named it, was its eventual splashdown within Hastings' store itself, where it sat surrounded by thirty RGD television sets on the outside while the inside housed a television lounge. Lady Barnett was there to present a closed-circuit TV show, and the thirty TV sets gave Hastings' shoppers a sample of what TV commercials were all about.

The public were also to receive autographs and souvenir pieces of cake. The whole affair must have out-Busbyed Berkeley, yet RGD has been swallowed up – and today Hastings' store is somebody else's.

But perhaps the peak of originality and the elephant's eye of lunacy was the sales pitch of the 'Talking Aeroplane' people. Operating the only aircraft fitted with loudspeaker equipment in the UK, the 'Talking Aeroplane' would

Overleaf: The greatest might-have-beens in the history of 'television' advertising.

IN BARS

LOUNGES

CANTEENS

CLUBS

TELEPOSTERS put you in the
TV picture for **10/-** a week

Wherever people foregather to wait, to chat, to eat, or have a friendly pint, a television set becomes the magnet, the one point in the room that draws all eyes. **That is the point where your advertisement ought to be, and where it now can be!**
Superb H.M.V. 17″ television sets are being installed at many indoor points where crowds can be guaranteed. Each set is handsomely mounted and built-in, and is surrounded, at eye level, by 15 advertising panels. **These panels, each measuring 10″ x 8″, are now being let to advertisers.** You can put your message in colour next to the TV screen in popular bars, air terminals, waiting lounges, canteens and clubs.
Teleposter sites are rated as follows:
CLASS A sites with weekly viewership of 5,000 and
upward 10/- a week
CLASS B sites with weekly viewership of 3,000 and
upward 6/- a week

CLASS C sites with weekly viewership of 2,000 and
upward 4/- a week

National coverage will be available, or any particular area can be selected. The first 50 Teleposters will be installed by the end of January 1955, and a hundred more will be added each month in various parts of the country. Here is a remarkable new advertising medium reaching people in relaxed and receptive mood, and at very low cost.

Get the full Teleposter story from the General Manager: W. Anderson, Teleposters Ltd, 30 Southampton Buildings, Chancery Lane, London, W.C.2 (Holborn 2747)

Teleposters are being developed by the above company in association with Bateman's Advertising Service, and by arrangement with The Gramophone Co. Ltd.

Advertising on TV still wrapped in mystery, but advertising <u>next</u> to TV is here — and here to stay!

Tremendous interest in Teleposters

The public aren't waiting for commercial TV with bated breath. They're looking at television **now**, and wise advertisers are going to make use of that steady gaze!

For thousands will soon be looking at public TV sets installed in bars, waiting lounges, clubs and canteens by Teleposters Ltd. Each set will be built-in and surrounded by 15 advertisement panels.

No 'outdoor' or posting campaign in 1955 will be complete without the Teleposter sites, each of which will give you a fascinated viewership **at the rate of 2/- a week per thousand.**

The first 50 Teleposters will be installed by the end of this month and hundreds more will follow. There is tremendous interest wherever a Teleposter is installed, and this is reflected among agencies and advertisers who see this as a new way to reach people in a receptive mood at low cost.

Get full details from the General Manager : W. Anderson, Teleposters Ltd, 30 Southampton Buildings, Chancery Lane, London, W.C.2. (Holborn 2747).

Teleposters are being developed by the above company in association with Bateman's Advertising Service and by arrangement with The Gramophone Co. Ltd. (His Masters Voice).

The Savage SE5a just taking off on a skywriting trip was owned by the Savage Skywriting Company. The picture was taken at Hendon in 1928.

fly around the chosen target area literally shouting advertising messages from the sky at the people down below.

Aerial advertising fell into five categories, all subject to flying regulations:

1. **Banner towing** could only be done if the certificate of airworthiness of the aircraft expressly authorized it. In 1939 the Gorrell Committee recommended that no new authorizations for banner towing should be given after 1941, but this had been overruled on several occasions. (London Weekend Television tangled with this regulation in the 1970s when they wanted to tow their familiar 'World of Sport' banner between two planes to accompany the opening titles of the show; they eventually had to shoot the film in Holland.)

2. **Skywriting** was not controlled, but under rule 19 of *Rules of the Air*, 'Aerobatic Flight', this was forbidden over any town or populated area and over certain other parts of the country.

3. **Dropping leaflets** was forbidden under rule 17 of *Rules of the Air*, but permission was sometimes given if the material was to be dropped, with the permission of the occupiers, on enclosed land.

4. **Illuminated advertisements** could, with permission from the Minister, be allowed underneath the wings of an aeroplane.

5. **Sky shouting**, however, was completely free of regulations, although it had to be borne in mind that any private pilot flying over an occupier's

Ghost writing in the sky. A beautifully composed sky advertisement. Pilots trained for skywriting on bicycles – tracing letters in reverse on the airfield in order to work out the manoeuvres that would be required once skyborne.

land could be termed a trespasser, since the occupier of the land also owned the air above it and as far upwards as the eye could see.

The business of shouting slogans from the sky was a tricky one, with unexpected hazards. No one in the business had forgotten the incident in 1932 when an aeroplane advertising Batchelor's peas was flown over crowds observing the two-minute silence on Armistice Day. According to reports, the public reaction was 'immediate and unfavourable'. Batchelors immediately terminated the contract with the 'Talking Aeroplane' company, took rapid legal action against them and received substantial damages for their resulting loss of trade.

However, before advertising *on* the TV screen, at least one company made a last grab for the TV advertising market – advertising all round the TV screen. There is a naïve poignancy about their series of full-page advertisements in the trade press in the spring of 1955 – and also a marvellous innocence about their view of things to come, based primarily on Teleposter's premise that television would remain a communal form of entertainment instead of the ordinary piece of domestic furniture it became.

The Teleposter's pitch symbolizes, in retrospect, the last bridge between the familiar world in which advertisers had lived and moved since the days of the travelling medicine show and some strange new planet where no one was very certain about what kind of life-support system was needed.

PART 3

'Another Opening, Another Show'

Countdown to ITV

The advertising business is like no other in that it combines two seemingly irreconcilable qualities – action and inertia. Of all the established 'professions', advertising is the most vulnerable to external change. It is a chameleon, needing 360-degree vision and the ability to colour itself to new surroundings immediately.

Almost as if to cloak themselves in security and impress the world with their solidity, advertising agencies outdo even the legal profession in the very names they are known by – Masius, Wynne-Williams & D'Arcy-Macmanus is consistently in the top agency listings, as are Ogilvy Benson & Mather; Collett, Dickenson, Pearce & Partners; Wasey-Campbell-Ewald; and Davidson, Pearce, Berry & Spottiswoode. Beside these the names of Lintas and even J. Walter Thompson are masterpieces of understatement. But for every simple agency title there are a dozen in the style of Medcalf, Wrightson, Lovelock, Kenyon & Eckhardt; Boase Massimi Pollitt Univas Partnership; Foote Cone & Belding; and Doyle Dane Bernbach. The names resound and have weight and authority, but paradoxically that authority is totally dependent on the advertisers' confidence in the agency's ability to shift his wares. This leaves the agency in the unenviable situation of being both master and servant, owning and owned. Which goes a long way towards explaining why despite the many years of debate over the subject of commercial television in Britain, and the final victory of the pro-commercial lobby, the advertising agencies were astonishingly unprepared to cope with the new medium and largely ignorant of its potential. Added to this was the kind of disdain that only British gentlefolk can hold with utter conviction for something they regard as slightly 'infra-dig'. Commercial television might have been all very well for the 'Americans', with their brash ways and uninhibited, shameless selling methods. But the 'British' way was not loud and not obvious.

The British way was typified by the 1955 National Radio Show, which was held at Earl's Court between 24 August and 3 September – less than a month before the day of the first commercial television transmission. The then Radio Industry Council, after some consideration, gave notice to the advertising agencies in the week of 21 July that it would offer facilities for

commercial TV films to be shown at its exhibition the following month. Rates were to be £50 for one-minute films, £30 for half a minute and £20 for twenty-five seconds. Agents' commission of 15% was to 'be allowed'. Advertising space was to be allotted by ballot to all suitable applicants, except to firms engaged in the manufacture of radio, which were expressly forbidden to take television advertising space during the National Radio Show!

Compensation for this curious holding back from the new medium came from the most unexpected quarters. The British Trawlers Federation and its agents – Dolan, Davies, Whitcombe & Stewart – had waded in with the bravura production of nine commercial television spots – four of fifteen seconds, four of thirty seconds and one sixty seconder. All nine were produced over a three-day period at Rotherhithe Studios, where a replica of the bridge of a typical British trawler had been built. The report of this marathon shooting session ends with the information that Rotherhithe Studios would be taking two weeks' holiday, after which they would be making several more 'commercial television productions'.

While the British Trawlers Federation were getting on with their unique

A location shoot for an early road-safety commercial sponsored by Regent Petrol. Far side of the camera is director Ray Elton. Opposite him is Anthony Shaffer. The camera was a clockwork Newman-Sinclair which could run for just two minutes after it had been wound.

contribution to television advertising, most of the major advertising agencies were juggling with the advice that was coming at them from all quarters. There was advice about the 'commentaries' on commercials from Guy Presbury, a director of Presbury's Screen Advertising Association, who did not think commentaries 'should be changed for various stations'. There was no need to use a northern accent for a northern station, he explained, drawing from his experience of cinema advertising throughout Great Britain, and concluded that he was 'convinced that commentaries should be in "pure" English and not regionally accented'.

Advertisers Weekly, the advertising trade paper which in 1955 had the highest weekly sale of any journal devoted to British advertising and marketing, published guidelines on television advertising as a service to its readers:

Product demonstrations must be believable

DO keep demonstrations simple and believable. Be honest in the actual demonstration, without camera tricks or exaggerated results. Work in closeups when possible so that the viewer learns by example how to use the product correctly.

The demonstrator must have authority

DO cast for believability. Often it is wise to use the older housewife in "example" selling. Authority begins at 40.

Where the shoe might pinch

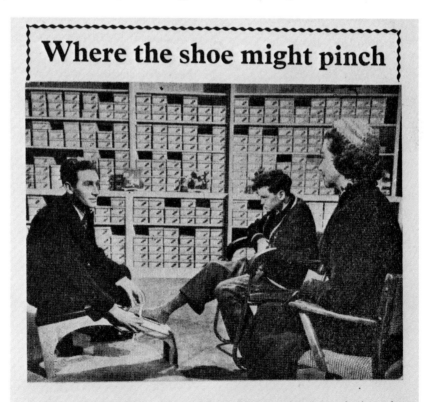

A scene from a film ("The Story of Johnny Blair"), made for television transmission, to advertise shoes by C. & J. Clark Ltd. Live action is considered most suitable for such "serious" products and a "must" for products where quality counts.

Wild claims look absurd on TV

DON'T make wild claims you cannot prove. TV exaggerates the exaggerated claim—more than any other medium—and makes it ridiculous.

The

singing

jingle

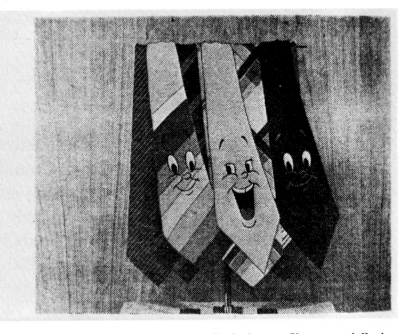

DO expect to repeat a singing jingle in any films, especially in cartoon. This tie spot ran intermittently in the US for four years. Viewers do not quickly tire of music and animation, except in saturation campaigns, where repeated too often, too soon.

Never take risks with tradition

DON'T try to extract comedy from established traditional concepts. Never risk being offensive with things "sacred" to viewers.

Use the kitchen for believability

DO use familiar settings. This breakfast table and kitchen are within the desire-believability of the average viewer.

Make the domestic scene realistic

DON'T use settings beyond the experience of the viewer. In TV, the mind does not have time to orient itself to the unusual setting, then grasp the message. This scene was intended to show the housewife playing bridge with the time she saved by using the washing machine.

The earliest commercials relied mainly on the talent of the British film industry. But James Garrett, a former director of TVA, recalled the antagonism which his company faced at the beginning from a film industry which considered work in commercials as 'treachery'. The film studios at Pinewood and Shepperton refused to offer a variation in the normal tariff to makers of commercials, which meant in the early years that TVA was saddled with the expense of a minimum studio hire of two to three days (when one would have been enough) and payment of the studio-supplied crew.

This determined Garrett to become self-sufficient in filming facilities when he left TVA and founded his own production company. TVA eventually crashed, but not before Garrett had given Karel Reisz his first-ever commercial to direct. Reisz is in distinguished company as a director of TV commercials. According to John Schlesinger, every major British director except David

I T A

INDEPENDENT TELEVISION PROGRAMMES
WILL COMMENCE SOON FROM
THE NEW I T A TRANSMITTING STATION
DESIGNED TO SERVE YOUR AREA

THIS IS A PILOT TRANSMISSION ON LOW POWER
TO HELP DEALERS INSTALL BAND III AERIALS
AND ADJUST SETS NOW AND SO REDUCE DELAYS
AND DISAPPOINTMENTS WHEN PROGRAMMES BEGIN

I T A

MILES
1 2 3 4 5 6

RECEPTION
REPORTS MAY
BE SENT TO:—
I T A ENG. DIV.
14 PRINCES GATE
LONDON, S.W.7.

THE WAVY LINE
IS TO SHOW UP
DELAYED IMAGES
(GHOSTS) WHICH
MAY APPEAR ON
THE BLACK OR
WHITE STRIPS.
THE DOTS ENABLE
AN ESTIMATE
OF THE DELAY
DISTANCES
TO BE MADE.

PILOT TEST TRANSMISSION

Two of the earliest ITA Test Cards, which capture the sense of anticipation of an alternative to the BBC.

Lean has directed commercials. American feature film directors, on the other hand, seem to have absolutely nothing to do with television advertising films.

The following directors have all worked on commercials during the last twenty-five years – listed too are examples of campaigns they have been involved in.

Lindsay Anderson: Ewbank carpet sweepers; Iron Jelloids; Picnic; Guinness; Kellogg's cornflakes.

Kevin Billington: Cussons Imperial Leather Soap; Stork margarine.

John 'Paddy' Carstairs: Wonderloaf.

Clive Donner: Kellogg's Special K; Ribena.

Cy Endfield: Lifebuoy soap.

Stephen Frears: Whitbread Trophy; Harp lager; Co-op.

Jack Gold: Fiat cars; Hamlet cigars; Silvikrin shampoo; Moulinex; Wrigley's gum.

Dick Lester: Smarties; Polos; Andrex.

Joseph Losey: Ryvita; Horlicks.

Joe McGrath: Watneys; White's lemonade.

Midge McKenzie: Milk of Magnesia.

Alan Parker: Birdseye beefburgers.

Karel Reisz: Persil; Knorr; Mars bars; Chanel 19; Campari; Kraft Cracker Barrel.

Ken Russell: Black Magic.

John Schlesinger: Stork margarine; Enos fruit salts; Polos; Black Magic; Kraft Cracker Barrel.

Ridley Scott: Hovis.

Anthony Simmons: Persil; Kellogg's; Findus; Martini; Beecham's Powders.

Claude Whatham: Weetabix: *The Observer*: Fairy Liquid.

Peter Yates: North British Rubber

Mai Zetterling: Persil

Theatre director Joan Littlewood once directed a campaign for the British Egg Marketing Board. Starring Avis Bunnage and George Sewell, the producer was Anthony Shaffer, and one of the cameramen was Nicolas Roeg. TVA, the film production company, took a full-page advertisement in *Television Mail* (5 June 1964) to announce its release. As can be seen from the wording of the advertisement, the campaign was regarded as something of a breakthrough.

Twenty-five years ago the British film industry feared the worst from commercial television. Now it has much to thank it for.

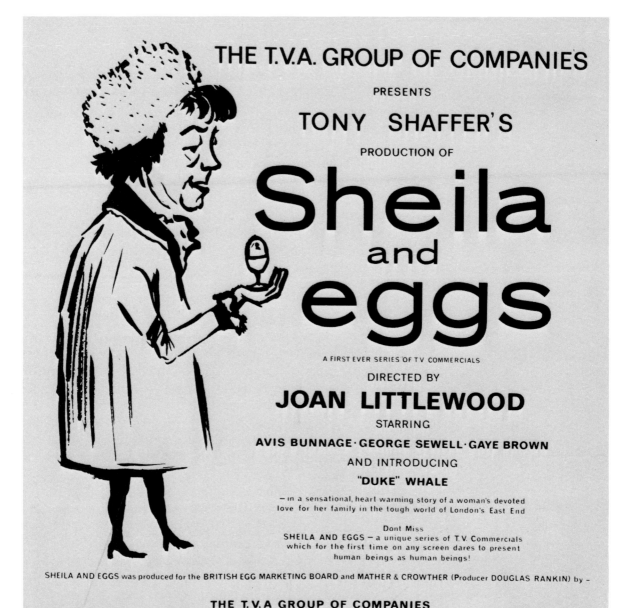

THE T.V.A. GROUP OF COMPANIES

PRESENTS

TONY SHAFFER'S

PRODUCTION OF

Sheila
and
eggs

A FIRST EVER SERIES OF TV COMMERCIALS

DIRECTED BY

JOAN LITTLEWOOD

STARRING

AVIS BUNNAGE · GEORGE SEWELL · GAYE BROWN

AND INTRODUCING

"DUKE" WHALE

– in a sensational, heart warming story of a woman's devoted
love for her family in the tough world of London's East End

Dont Miss
SHEILA AND EGGS – a unique series of T.V. Commercials
which for the first time on any screen dares to present
human beings as human beings!

SHEILA AND EGGS was produced for the BRITISH EGG MARKETING BOARD and MATHER & CROWTHER (Producer DOUGLAS RANKIN) by –

THE T.V.A GROUP OF COMPANIES

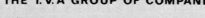

DIRECTOR	JOAN LITTLEWOOD
PRODUCER	TONY SHAFFER
ART DIRECTOR	EDWIN FLORENCE
CAMERAMEN	DAVID WATKINS
	& NICOLAS ROEG
CAMERA OPERATOR	GEOFFREY SEAHOLME
EDITOR	DAVID HOWES

This series of commercials had feature film-style billing in the trade press of June 1964.

By Thursday evening of 22 September 1955 an estimated two million people, mainly in the London area, were ready and waiting to watch the first night of Independent Television. ABC Television (later ATV) and Associated Rediffusion – the two companies responsible for the production of the first night's programmes – were about to meet this first audience, whose television sets had been converted to receive the new wavelength via Channel 9 beamed from the ITA's only transmitter, which was housed in a temporary building in Croydon. The Croydon station had been built by the Marconi Company in less than nine months and its temporary nature, although a matter of chance, certainly reflected the touch-and-go atmosphere surrounding the evening of the 22nd. Nevertheless, twenty-four advertisers demonstrated their faith in the new medium and shortly after eight o'clock – at seven seconds after 8.12 pm precisely – pioneer DJ and BBC radio and TV star Jack Jackson, who was compering a starry variety bill, turned to camera and announced, 'Now – the moment you've all been waiting for.' British television's first commercial hit the watching thousands, thereby achieving a place in TV history simply by the luck of the draw (it had been decided beforehand that the fairest way of allocating television time to the first twenty-four advertisers was to draw lots for the running order, and Gibbs SR toothpaste won). For the record, the other twenty-three were Guinness, Batchelor's peas, Brillo, Cadburys, Crosse & Blackwell, Dunlop Rubber, Esso, Ford, Remington Rand, Shredded Wheat, Surf, Watneys, National Benzole, Kraft cheese, Woman, Coty, Brown & Polson, Express Dairy Co, Crompton lamps, Lux, Summer County margarine, E. K. Cole – manufacturers of Ecko radio and television sets, and Oxo.

But the first sixty seconds belong to Gibbs SR, and along with the striking visual of a tube of SR embedded in a block of ice (the use of a real ice-block had to be abandoned after several unsuccessful experiments and the final effect was achieved with plastic and hours of painstaking work at the Pathé Studios in Wardour Street), and accompanied by a soundtrack of gently running water mixed with a matching flute and violin orchestration, went the words – 140 of them – spoken in finest 'BBC English' by Alex Mackintosh, a well-known BBC presenter at the time.

> It's tingling fresh.
> It's fresh as ice.
> It's Gibbs SR Toothpaste, the tingling fresh toothpaste that does your gums good too.
> The tingle you get when you brush with SR is much more than a nice taste – it's a tingle of health. It tells you something very important, that you're doing your gums good and toughening them to resist infection.

The first ever TV commercial opening shot – *Trompe d'oeil* triumph. The running water, all 400 gallons, had to be siphoned into the studio's 'gents'.

Ten years before the 'ice-block'.

(Cut from ice-block to chart)

And, as this chart shows, gum infection is the cause of more tooth losses than decay itself.

The tingle in SR comes from Sodium Ricinoleate – a substance which both dental research and years of use in dental practice have shown to be good for the gums.

So to keep your teeth white as snow, your gums really healthy and your breath really fresh, see your dentist regularly and brush with SR – the tingling fresh toothpaste for teeth and gums.

Gibbs SR.

The words remain a classic example of the earnest, informative but also fanciful style that was adopted in so many early commercials. The ice-block was a brilliant concept, perfectly in harmony with the 'tingling freshness' aspect of the toothpaste, but excess of words eventually overrode the picture. The music track was hesitant, meandering and inconsequential, as if the music had been an afterthought, and the sound of running water was again at odds with the all-important packshot of the block of ice and the first-ever person to appear in a television commercial.

At this point it is worth remembering that television commercials had a relatively tiny audience compared with the national press in 1955. In 1956 it had a potential audience of 60% of the population but people could only receive ITV if they had their existing sets converted, or bought new ones capable of receiving Channel 9.

Never ignore a speck of blood on your toothbrush. Gum-bleeding is the first sign of gum-rot. *See your dentist immediately.* Sodium Ricinoleate is well known among dentists as the best home treatment for gum troubles, and that's why it's in " S.R." Toothpaste. Use " S.R." daily to promote sound teeth and healthy gums.

Have no doubt about healthy gums—protect gums as well as teeth with

S.R.

TOOTHPASTE

1/3 *(including tax)*

SR 142-974-55   D. & W. GIBBS LIMITED, E.C.4

In order of opening and transmission area the programme companies were:

Associated Rediffusion	London weekdays	22/9/55
Associated Broadcasting Company (later ATV)	London weekends Midlands weekdays	24/9/55
Associated British Picture Corporation	Midlands weekends	18/2/56

(Associated British Cinemas took Associated Broadcasting Company to court over the use of the initials ABC on its call-sign. The companies settled out of court and Associated Broadcasting Company changed its name to Associated TeleVision Ltd in October 1955).

Scottish Television	Central Scotland	31/8/57
Television Wales & West	South Wales and West of England	14/1/58
Southern Television	South of England	30/8/58
Tyne Tees Television	North-East England	15/1/59
Anglia Television	East of England	27/10/59
Ulster Television	Northern Ireland	31/10/59
Westward Television	South-West England	29/4/61
Border Television	Borders	1/9/61
Channel Television	Channel Islands	1/9/62
Wales West & North	West Wales & North Wales	14/9/62
Border Television	Isle of Man	26/3/65
HTV (taking over from WWN & TWW)	Wales & West of England	4/3/68
Thames Television (taking over from Associated Rediffusion)	London weekdays	29/7/68
London Weekend Television (taking over from ATV)	London weekends	2/8/68
Yorkshire Television	Yorkshire	29/7/68

This distribution of programme companies in major cities throughout the country achieved the ITA's aim of offering a completely regional service, and meant greater opportunities for coverage of local news and advertising.

A once familiar sight, the Rediffusion clock known fondly as 'Mitch' after Leslie Mitchell, who presented the opening ceremonial on ITV's first night.

In days of higher employment local factories frequently used television to advertise for staff. Regional tastes in food could also be catered for. Canned food in general and processed peas in particular have always been more popular in the North, as have wrapped bread, jam and chocolate biscuits. The South, on the other hand, was quicker to take up frozen foods, fabric conditioners and kitchen paper rolls.

Above all, regional television was to take the focus off London, which had commanded the television scene for so long.

PART 4
'Who Were You With Last Night'
BBC or ITV

Britain's first night of commercial television was given an enthusiastic reception by most of the daily press, but only now, twenty-five years later, can it be revealed that quite unwittingly ITV caused the demise of a radio heroine on the night of 22 September. The irony of the whole affair was that had it not been for an American commercial television invention – the endless family serial usually sponsored by a soap company and nicknamed a soap opera – BBC radio might never have had a long-running serial that could command a devoted audience of eight million for its fifteen minutes' spot at 6.45 pm every evening.

'The Archers' – still running today – meant a lot more to its listeners then. They had been brought up on radio entertainment, and its only real rivals for attention were two less exciting radio alternatives. BBC television did not broadcast between 6 and 7 in the evening until 1957. 'The Archers' episode of the previous night had ended on an untypical cliffhanger but it was, nevertheless, an event that could well have happened in an 'everyday story of country folk', as it used to be billed. Grace Archer – married only the previous year to Philip – had dashed into a blazing stable to rescue a horse. The faithful tuned in on Thursday the 22nd anxious to hear of her rescue, but Grace, far from being rescued, was trapped by a falling beam, dragged out by Philip and was dead before she reached hospital. Stunned by the loss, millions wept quietly at home, while others kept the BBC switchboard occupied for hours that evening just asking 'Why'?

Some newspapers hinted at the coincidence, but it had never been confirmed until a scriptwriter involved in 'The Archers' scripts for the months leading up to ITV's opening night admitted during researches for this book that Grace Archer's death and the events leading up to it were coolly calculated – months in advance – to take the spotlight off the new television service. The plan succeeded dramatically, but 'Auntie' BBC – that comfortable nickname – seems an inappropriate description for someone who sacrificed a member of her own family because she didn't want all her nephews and nieces to play with somebody else.

Perhaps it was poetic justice that ITV, including the advertising 'bits', started off so well. It was too early in the life of television commercials for

First Plug Girl

Meet Meg

KETCH
2d

...Y, SEPTEMBER 23, 1955

...reign Secretary Macmillan
...on Burgess and Maclean

A HALO
...OR THE
...O. STAFF

...HAROLD MAC-
...MILLAN made
...ut defence of
...ign Office staff
...y over the Bur-
...nd Maclean

"...most loyal,
...efficient, most
...d body of men"
...d them.

...most the same
...s Lord John
...s joint under-
...o, he declared

that if there were any
mistakes they were the
mistakes of Ministers.

Mr. Macmillan was speak-
ing at a lunch of the
Foreign Press Association
in London.

He was asked: "Is any-
body at the Foreign Office
to blame for the Burgess
and Maclean affair?

With a smile he replied:
"It is too easy, you know.
You ought to have had 30
years on Tees-side as I
have."

He was formerly M.P. for
Stockton-on-Tees.

Then, referring to the
circumstances in which

the two Foreign Office
men vanished behind the
Iron Curtain four years
ago, he said:

"The answer is that I
am the responsible person
and I have no doubt I
shall be blamed.

"I wish to take this
opportunity of saying,
which I think needs say-
ing, that we have the good
fortune in this country to
be served by the most
loyal and most efficient
Foreign Service, at home
and abroad, that any
country could have.

"I want to make it doubly
clear that, if there are mistakes, they are the mistakes
of Ministers.

NOTHING COULD
BE WORSE

"Nothing could be worse
than for me to do anything
which would undermine the
confidence of the Foreign
Service itself and the confidence of our people in the
Foreign Service.

"If Ministers were to try
to shelter from their re-
sponsibilites they would not
be doing their duty by the
most splendid body of men
whom any Minister could
have to serve him."

Mr. Macmillan empha-

→ **Back Page**

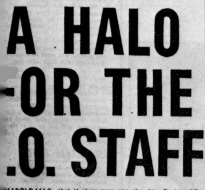

SHE stepped into radio history last night—
by becoming the first person to appear in
an advertisement on British TV. Her name:
Meg Smith.

Viewers of ITV's star-studded opening programme saw her cleaning her teeth in a 60-

second film for Gibbs S.R. Toothpaste. To become Britain's first plug girl, Meg—height
5ft. 4in., bust 34in., waist 23in., hips 35in.—
beat 80 other actresses and models. She knew
the recommended "up-and-down-and-round-
the-gums" toothbrush routine.

*Simply
wonderful*

THESE
...RILLO SOAP PADS

The first 'Plug Girl'
shares the morning
after's front page with a
tale continued and still
not ended.

Below left: Grace Archer
dominates the *Daily
Mirror's* front page.

Below: The moving
inside story of the night
fans wept in the streets.

She is
DEAD,
'killed'
by the
B.B.C.

THOUSANDS mourned
last night for
GRACE ARCHER (left),
a girl who exists only in
radio fiction. . . .

She "DIED" tragic-
ally in yesterday even-
ing's episode of the popular B.B.C. series, "The
Archers"—and her death
roused a storm of protest
from listeners.

Full story—Page 8.

RADIO FANS WEPT AS
GRACE ARCHER 'DIED'

DAILY MIRROR REPORTER

THE B.B.C.
"killed" off
Grace Archer—one
of the best-known
characters of their
radio series, "The
Archers" — last
night. . . . AND
ARCHER FANS
WEPT IN THE
STREETS.

In Wednesday even-
ing's episode Grace
Archer dashed into a
blazing stable to rescue
a horse.

**IN MY ARMS . . . ON
THE WAY TO HOSPITAL
. . . SHE'S DEAD."**

The programme ended—
and the storm broke.

The serial's nightly

audience of 8,000,000
turned on their sets at
6.45 p.m. yesterday ex-
pecting to hear of her
escape. . .

Instead, they heard she
had been trapped by a
falling beam.

There was a stunned
silence in homes through-
out Britain as Phil Archer
—"married" to her only a
few months ago — stam-
mered tragically:

In Wednesday even-
ing's episode Grace
Archer dashed into a

phoned the B.B.C. A B.B.C.
spokesman said: "There
were continual calls from
listeners for well over an
hour.

"Calls were still coming
through two hours after
the programme ended."

And Miss Angela Hoyle,
of Broad Mead - road,
Folkestone, told me: "On
my way from Ashford to
Dover tonight I spoke to a
number of people who were
openly weeping for Grace
Archer.

"I was travelling by
car, and as I passed
through villages I saw
people standing at their
doors in tears.

"I stopped again and

again. Everywhere the
story was the same.

"In pubs, cafes and out-
side their doors people were
crying over Grace Archer.

"One family I spoke to
on Romney Marsh were
COLLECTING FLOWERS
to make into wreaths and
crosses to send to the
funeral.

"I met a trainee nurse
in tears because, she said,
'only last Monday
Grace Archer announced
she was going to start a
family.'"

Upset

Mr. Keith Waller, of Il-
ford, Essex, said: "The
emotional level of the ending was disgraceful.

"My mother—who is not
over-sensitive — was quite
upset."

Another listener, Mrs. E.
Mitchell, of Childeric-road,
New Cross, said: "These
characters may be fictional,
but people have grown to

love them. Grace's death
was a shock."

All who phoned their pro-
tests to the B.B.C. and
newspapers asked the same
question:

WHY DID IT HAVE TO
HAPPEN?

Mr. Edward J. Mason,
one of the programme's
script writers, gave me the
answer:

"Grace's death was de-
cided on to maintain the
serial's realistic aspect."

The part of Grace has
been played by actress
Ysanne Churchman since
February, 1952.

Hundreds of Archer fans
attended her "wedding"
last Easter to Philip—
played by Norman Paint-
ing—when the programme
was recorded at a church
at Hanbury Worcs.

Last night she com-
mented: "I am very sorry
so many people are miser-
able about the death of
Grace Archer.

IT WAS NO WISH OF
MINE. . . . I have enjoyed
taking the part."

them to have a generic title, which left the next mornings' press in a dilemma. Most got round it by using several different names for the same thing, but the most popular term – used by the *Daily Express, Manchester Guardian, Daily Mirror, Daily Sketch, Daily Telegraph, Financial Times* and *Daily Worker* – was 'advertisements'. Six used 'plugs' – the *Daily Express, Daily Mirror, Evening News, Daily Sketch, Daily Worker* and *News Chronicle*. Another six used the word 'commercials' – of them only one did not hedge its bets with any other description – the *Daily Herald, Daily Mail, Daily Mirror, Daily Worker, Daily Telegraph* and *News Chronicle*. Two also used the word 'adverts' – the *Daily Mirror* and *Daily Worker. The Daily Telegraph* went for 'announcements' as another choice. The *Mail* chose 'ads' and *The Financial Times* referred to 'advertisement items'. 'Commercials' and 'ads' have both stayed the course, with 'adverts' and 'advertisements' also being quite widely used. Strangely, no one word has emerged as truly definitive.

The public took to ITV from the first night. A Gallup Poll commissioned by the *News Chronicle* showed that nearly one in five television sets in the London area was tuned to the early programmes on ITV, and that on average four people (of whom one was a visitor) looked in on each set. For every two people looking at ITV, five were tuned to the BBC; and of those who watched ITV, two in every three thought it had got off to a good start; one in ten was critical; the rest had not formed an opinion.

What did take the viewers by surprise was the number and timing of the 'natural breaks'. There had never been an unequivocal statement about what a 'natural break' in the programmes really meant, although it had been generally assumed that these breaks would be at the beginning and end of every programme. In practice it was soon discovered that natural breaks could be within the programmes themselves. This caused a degree of embarrassment for advertisers with space between the rounds in a televised boxing match that night. At one point the commentator was just exclaiming, 'Now the other boy's nose is bleeding too', when the picture was replaced with an ad (for Guinness) showing a seal waddling across the screen with a glass of stout balanced on its nose. 'My goodness', yelled the zookeeper then on screen, but the exclamation was more like a reply to the commentator.

Another beer commercial was even more badly placed. It showed a row of tumblers (full of Watneys beer) emptying themselves unaided while the offscreen voice said, 'You try it.' The picture then cut back to the boxing match just as one of the contestants was spitting uninhibitedly into a bucket.

Spotting unintentional humour like this added a dimension to early commercial television watching, and the occasional funny juxtaposition did more to endear than annoy.

Pilchard à la Peggy Lee. A star was canned. Imagined and animated by Oscar Grillo and Sergio Simonetti of Dragon Productions.

LEFT The Dulux Dog: ICI Paints Division chose an appealing Old English sheepdog named Dash to give a more homely appearance to their room sets for paint commercials in 1964. He was such a success that Dulux kept him on for eight years. He was followed by Digby, winner of a competition to find a successor. Digby retired in 1978. Now Dillon has taken over the role, with occasional appearances by Woolly and Mr Kelly. But whatever their name, each one is, simply, the Dulux dog – a term that has become almost a synonym for the breed.

BELOW Arthur, the Kattomeat Cat: Arthur's mum wrote to Spillers in 1967 about how her cat ate tinned catfood with one paw. Spillers contacted Geers-Gross, the advertising agents, who arranged a screen test for this feline Spencer Tracy. He was such a success that Spillers bought him and lovingly cared for him – at various high-class catteries including Pussy Galore – for the rest of his life. He died at the age of fourteen in 1977 but his name lives on as No. 1 choice for white kittens.

LEFT The Black Horse: symbolizing power, the black horse would have appealed to D. H. Lawrence. The commercial was filmed in Cornwall in 1975 and directed by Gerry Poulson with a music track by Chris Gunning. It won the CLIO award in New York for world-wide advertising excellence in the 'International Television' category.

OPPOSITE The Esso Tiger: Wild, defiant and undeniably the most beautiful creature to appear in a television commercial. The face that decorates millions of walls also gives captive people a sense of freedom.

A rare and breathtaking use of landscape in this commercial for Evian mineral water. Shot by a French crew from a helicopter above the French Alps, the music, voiceover and images communicate the essence of the product.

19 May 1957 became a golden evening of laughter during one commercial break of two minutes and twenty-five seconds for viewers in Yorkshire. Because of a 'sound engineering slip-up' the wrong soundtrack accompanied the visuals, resulting in a series of commercials that ran thus:

VOICEOVER:	'Clean your teeth with this' –
	Visual – a sausage
VOICEOVER:	'Give this to your cat' –
	Visual – a bottle of Babycham
	'It will love it' –
VOICEOVER:	'This will make your hair gleam' –
	Visual – a tube of toothpaste
VOICEOVER:	'Lubricate your car with this' –
	Visual – a bottle of beer

Finally a well-fed cat was shown. 'That's my husband,' said the voiceover.

Poor ABC-TV, the station then transmitting to Yorkshire. No one will ever know the real reason for that mistake – perhaps it was the work of a sound man with an offbeat sense of humour, because the same thing happened two months later during a shorter break when just two commercials were shown.

VOICEOVER:	'There's nothing like this . . .'
	Visual – a spoonful of baked beans
VOICEOVER	'. . . in a glass of water when you're
	feeling under the weather' –

and to a shot of a packet of starch. VOICEOVER: 'Spread more on your bread.'

The revenue from the opening night to the programme contractors ABC and Rediffusion was £24,000, which was to be handed over to charities nominated by the Lord Mayor of London. In the event 12,000 guineas (!) was given to various charities in March 1956.

The chairman of the Independent Television Authority was then Sir Kenneth Clark. He had been interviewed the previous December for American television by Eric Sevareid and was asked to give his views on American TV commercials. 'They're a pretty mixed lot,' he told Sevareid. 'There are some amusing ones, especially the cartoons. But there are some that are a bit too insistent, for us at any rate. I wonder how well all that banging on the nerves would work over here.' Sir Kenneth was soon to find out.

Sir Compton Mackenzie
advocating Horlicks. The
packshot was kept
respectfully distant and
shown separately.

An American opinion on early British television commercials was given by John Crosby in the *Washington Post*:

They were – I am forced to confess – fearfully British, and frightfully uninsistent. One of them opened with a hearty Briton saying, 'Hello there. I want to talk about penguins.' And talk about penguins he did – about small penguins that live off the coast of Africa, about King penguins who warm their eggs between their feet and about Imperial Penguins. 'And also the other kind of penguin,' he added diffidently, 'milk chocolate Penguins,' and he held up a bar. 'Biggest milk chocolate bar in Britain.'

A 1955 commercial goes even further in its self-effacement. Spoken to camera by Sir Compton McKenzie, it left the product name till the last possible second.

VOICEOVER: Sir Compton McKenzie
(*cut to Sir Compton*)
SIR COMPTON: Yes, I suppose most people who are asked what are the three essentials to perfect health nominate fresh air, exercise and sleep. I've never bothered much about the first two, but profound ample sleep has contributed more than anything to whatever success I've enjoyed in life.
    At the age of seventy-two I can still sleep the clock round when the body and mind need recuperation, and therefore I can still work for ten hours of continuous mental concentration when necessary.
    I believe that all my imaginative work is composed during deep sleep, but I am very seldom aware of dreaming.
    For me a worse ill than blindness of deafness would be sleeplessness.
VOICEOVER: As Sir Compton says, sound sleep is all important. Horlicks helps you get not just sleep but sound refreshing sleep.

This peculiarly British uninsistent attitude seems to be linked with that quality which is summed up in the expression 'British reserve', as if advertising products can not be separated from self-advertisement; or becoming obvious; or making a noise; or communicating with strangers. Perhaps it is also bound up with ambivalence about money. Significantly, the picture in terms of income from the end of the war in 1945 to 1955 reflected a much greater equality of earning power, with 12% of the population earning £800 and above each year and 65% earning between £300 and £799.

Uninsistent or not, commercials started at a time when there was money

Food MoF Facts

HOW TO GET THE NEW
RATION BOOK

CUT OUT THIS NOTICE AND KEEP IT BY YOU

The new Ration Book (with the next Clothing Book) will be issued from May 22nd onwards. It will be used for food purchases from July 23rd.

Getting your new Ration Book will be easier and quicker this year if everyone follows these simple directions. We have divided them into BEFORE, DURING and AFTER. Take these stages one at a time, and you will help to make the job of giving out even 45,000,000 books go with a swing.

 Before you can get your new Ration Book you must see that both your IDENTITY CARD and your PRESENT RATION BOOK are in order.

Your *Identity Card* should have been signed on the left-hand inside page. It should also have your present permanent address on it. If it has not, or if you have lost your card, go at once to your local National Registration Office (same address as the Food Office), taking your present Ration Book with you. Remember it's no good going to a ration book distribution centre if your Identity Card has been lost or is incorrect.

Page 3 of your PRESENT RATION BOOK has been left blank so far. This must be filled in now. *This page must not be cut out.* Next make sure that page 36 has the names and addresses of your retailers written or stamped in the spaces provided.

 During the time that the new books are being given out (May 22nd onwards), the posters in your Food Office area and advertisements in your local newspapers will tell you where and when to get your book. Remember that the poster to go by is the one in your own Food Office area. It will be shown in Post Offices, cinemas and elsewhere.

When you go to get your new Ration Book you must have your present Food Book and your Identity Card with you. *Anyone can fetch your new book for you if they take your old book and Identity Card.* All the books for a household can be collected at one time, even if the surnames are different. Other arrangements will be made for people who cannot possibly fetch or send for their new book at the proper time.

If you are an expectant mother and are due to go to the Food Office between May 22nd and July 23rd to get your green Ration Book renewed, you can get your new Ration Books at the same time and so save yourself a second journey. Holders of temporary (yellow) Identity Cards who have to apply for extension during this period can also get their Ration Books at the same time.

 After you have got your new book you must:
(1) Write your address and National Registration Number on the front cover of the Food Book and your name, address and National Registration Number on the front of the Clothing Book.
(2) Next remove the Clothing Book carefully and put it away in a safe place. You will not be able to use it before 1st August.
(3) Then, on page 5 of the Ration Book, write your name and address in Section A and your *present* milk retailer's name and address in Section B.

THE MINISTRY OF FOOD, LONDON, W.I. FOOD FACTS No. 202

1945, a hint of what rationing entailed.

to spend; when people wanted to replace household objects that had had to last through rationing and austerity; and when the government had to abolish the 'make do and mend' ethic in the interests of boosting production and consumption – therefore spending – of which advertising was an integral part.

And gradually little shop windows between nine and twelve inches high took their place in the corner of millions of sitting-rooms.

The height of austerity – mid-Forties press ad.

PART 5

'Oh Dear, What Can the Matter Be?'
Disenchantment Sets In

By 1957 television audiences were happily switched to Independent Television. From February of that year the oddly named 'toddlers' truce' – a nightly television closedown between 6 and 7 pm for the sake of tiny bedtimes – had been abolished. But there were pockets of bedrock resistance, sometimes melding into downright hatred, for the infant television service.

John Wilmot (later Lord Wilmot), Labour MP for Deptford talked of 'This nightly poison, advertising, in the homes of working people,' adding that 'the boosting of goods to the working class was against the national interest'.

The first two Commons questions since the beginning of ITV were put to Postmaster-General Dr Charles Hill in December 1955. Patrick Gordon Walker, Labour MP for Smethwick, asked what action was to be taken about the extension of 'natural breaks' in programmes, such as had occurred during the televising of a boxing match on 15 November when an advertisement had interrupted the boxing. Elaine Burton, Labour MP for Coventry South (now Baroness Burton of Coventry), asked why 'the insertion of an advertisement for Esso petrol had suddenly appeared in the middle of "Sportsview" on the night of 16 November'.

These were the first two spots in a rash of 'natural break' complaints that lasted into the early sixties.

In the run-up to ITV's first night, MPs had sought some clear definition of when television advertisements would be shown and what was meant by a 'natural break' in the programme. There had never been a satisfactory explanation, but there was a general understanding that in a boxing match, for example, the break between rounds would be a 'natural break'. Sir Edward Boyle, then Parliamentary Secretary for the Ministry of Supply, told the House in March 1955 that 'there would not be more than six advertisement periods in an hour'. But he could only inform MPs that these would be at the beginning or end of programmes or during 'natural breaks'.

This blurring of the question was a gift to the opponents of commercial television, of whom Christopher Mayhew, Labour MP for Woolwich East, Ness Edwards, Labout MP for Caerphilly, and Don Chapman, Labour MP for Birmingham Northfield, were the most vigilant and vocal.

A typical ABC Television ad designed to attract advertisers to the medium.

Opposite: ABC Television reminded shopkeepers of the power of TV advertising in 1959.

Mr. Clarke becomes a customer

Frank Clarke is a successful grocer in Bolton. (You remember Mrs. Potter? She's one of his customers.) At the weekend Mr. Clarke, like Mrs. Potter, enjoys nothing more than putting his feet up and watching TV. When he sees the commercials he's in . . .

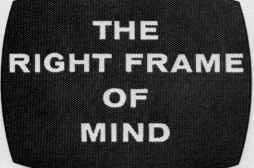

THE RIGHT FRAME OF MIND

That's common sense. We don't need psychologists to tell us that a man listens best when he can give his mind to it — when he has lots of free time and he's feeling happy and at ease.

So that when, on Monday morning, Mr. Clarke — the weekend customer — reverts to being a busy retailer, the lines he prefers to stock and display are the ones he's seen advertised regularly on TV — because he knows they'll go faster. That's common sense too.

THE ABC TELEVISION AREA covers the great industrial North and Midlands. That's half the independent television homes — and more than half all the grocers' shops — in England and Wales. The Mr. Clarkes, and the retailers of all kinds, who watch ABC are shrewd businessmen. They know the power of TV advertising. And they *see* that advertising with their own eyes at the weekend, when they're in the right frame of mind . . .

ABC TELEVISION NETWORK
Weekends in the North and Midlands

ABC TELEVISION LTD., 1 Hanover Square, London, W.1 · Tel: HYDE PARK 7222
A Member of the Associated British Picture Corporation

In February 1957 the Granada political discussion programme 'Under Fire' featured the greatly respected journalist Kingsley Martin, whose contribution was stopped in mid-sentence while a commercial for Tide was shown. In December 1958 'Under Fire' presented a discussion on capital punishment between Mr Gerald Gardiner QC (later Lord Gardiner) and a Mr W. J. Brown when the contributors were again interrupted by a commercial break. The programme proved aptly named, as both breaches were reported to the Commons with the request for action by Postmaster-General Ernest Marples to prosecute the ITA for breaking its law on 'natural breaks'. Granada announced soon after that 'Under Fire' would in future run without a break for commercials.

Soon after this, the case of a singer called 'Ivan', whose song 'Real Wild Child' had supposedly been halted in mid-note for a commercial break, was hoisted before the House of Commons as another infringement. Mr Marples answered this claim with the information that the song was not cut off for a 'break' but had an ending that repeated the phrase 'Wild Child' over and over, more and more faintly. Marples knew this, he said, because he 'had the record in his office at the House together with a gramophone'. He concluded by inviting any MP who wished to hear the song to take advantage of the facility.

The peccadillos continued. In January 1959, Christopher Mayhew drew the Postmaster-General's attention to the fact that a Mr Curtis, chairman of the Federation of Wholesale and Multiple Bakers, had been interrupted in mid-sentence while appearing on the 'This Week' programme – another intrusion of commercials. On 6 January, Mayhew continued, the play *The Bridge of San Luis Rey* had suffered two such interruptions and a premature ending – all for advertisements. (Just over a year before, the ITA had deferred to the eminence of Jean-Paul Sartre by televising his play *Men Without Shadows* without a single commercial break.)

However, television critic Milton Shulman wrote to *The Times* in March 1959 defending natural breaks. 'One man's nuisance is another man's delight,' he wrote.

> My own particular experience in TV leads me to believe that the vast bulk of the British public actually like the commercial breaks. Has anyone asked them? . . . Popular newspapers long ago discovered that 400 words was about the maximum that the average reader could take on any one subject. Translated into TV terms, I suspect that about fifteen continuous minutes is the maximum concentration effort of your normal viewer. He wants to put the cat out, brew some tea, go to the bathroom – without missing anything. Commercial breaks give him these opportunities. If

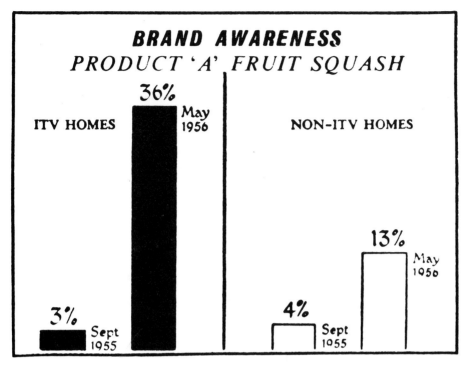

A 'Brand Awareness' survey conducted when a farthing was a coin of the realm.

anyone doubts the popularity of these advertising inserts, let him listen to the patter of any comic on the variety stage. Any reference to a jingle or a slogan made popular by commercial TV is greeted with delighted and affectionate laughter.

Shulman went on to challenge Mayhew's right to be a judge of what is a 'natural break' and asked, 'What would be his reaction if commercials were inserted in all of Shakespeare's natural breaks? *Hamlet* has no fewer than twenty of them.' (Mayhew had once said that he would accept a playwright's definition of a natural break.)

Shulman then asked whether the BBC was any better because it used the clock as an arbiter of natural breaks. 'Has Mr Mayhew never heard the BBC Brains Trust arbitrarily interrupted in the middle of a fascinating discussion to make way for something like Sooty?'

The 'natural break' argument raged well into the sixties, and Parliament witnessed other voices, other rows.

The British Trawlers Federation made news in 1957 by being refused space for a commercial which they wanted to place with Associated-

Rediffusion. The company refused the BTF because the commercial was to advertise a BBC-TV documentary. A-R had actually telephoned the Federation's advertising agent, Patrick Dolan, under the impression that the commercial script was a joke. Dolan assured them it was absolutely genuine but they refused to pass the script, saying it would be 'detrimental to the interests of other advertisers who had booked space for the programmes that would be broadcast at the same time as the advertised BBC documentary'.

Describing Rediffusion's attitude as 'ridiculous', Dolan added that there was a precedent in newspapers that accepted copy and advertisements from competing newspapers to advertise special features. 'If the newspapers have got the courage and independence to do this, surely Independent Television should do the same thing,' he said. 'It seems crazy for ITV to take the attitude that the BBC does not exist.'

The British Trawlers Federation finally obtained space for a commercial. It featured Anthony Fell, Conservative MP for Great Yarmouth (who was to have done the original version), and Norman Pierce, an actor who had taken part in another fishing industry film that was showing in ABC cinemas. This gave Pierce the opportunity to say in all honesty he had been working 'on a feature about the life of distant water trawlermen'.

A spokesman for the agency told *The Times* that they had hoped that the allusion to a 'feature', without any mention of its origin or where it could be seen, would be understood by the viewing public to refer to the BBC programme, although of course it was a different feature. The agency had tried, before engaging Norman Pierce, to obtain a cast list from the BBC from which they could have found an actor to appear in the commercial who would also be in the BBC programme. Such words bring a new dimension to 'devastating honesty'.

In July 1959, Don Chapman claimed his first battle honours. He forwarded a letter to the Postmaster-General from a Mrs P. Cole who had outlined three instances of misleading commercials. Chapman had insisted that the 'extravagant' product claims be investigated by the ITA. They were, and the ITA replied for each.

First was the case of Hovis, which advertised as having 'eight times more wheatgerm than ordinary brown bread – Then Hovis is eight times better.' The ITA saw little cause for concern in the context of 'this humorous little advertisement' but 'felt that on a strict interpretation of the principles for television advertising, the question and answer constituted a claim that could not be substantiated.'

The next for consideration, 'Maltesers, seven times less fattening than the centres of ordinary chocolates', was not objected to by the ITA.

In the third case, Shell-Mex and BP claimed that by using BP Energol

ATV sends Gumption sales soaring—372% in the Midlands, 154% in London

ATV advertising for Gumption household cleanser began in London on March 3rd and in the Midlands on March 13th, 1956. After only two weeks' advertising with 30-second "real-life" commercials there was a noticeable increase in sales. By May, two months later, sales in London and the Home Counties were 154% higher and in the Midlands *372% higher* than at the same time last year.

This success is, moreover, wholly attributed to advertising on ATV, because Gumption sales in non-ITV areas were by comparison up only 8%.

Advertising Agents for Gumption Products Ltd.
R. S. CAPLIN LTD.

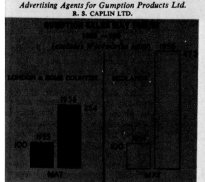

ATV—PROGRAMME CONTRACTORS FOR THE WEEKEND IN LONDON, AND MONDAY TO FRIDAY IN THE MIDLANDS

RICHARD ARBIB, *Managing Director of Gumption Products Ltd., states:*

"WE have previously undertaken specialized campaigns in the London area, employing newspapers, bus sides, and cards in tube trains, and although one such campaign cost more than double the amount we spent on television in two months, we did not achieve results which were at all comparable with those which we have recently experienced. As a company, Gumption is indeed very grateful for television.

"Whilst we have not, of course, yet made profit out of our recent television publicity, we believe from the recent large increase in sales that more and more housewives will use Gumption regularly in their homes, and ultimately television advertising will be proved to have been the most inexpensive publicity medium we have ever used."

For those who want further details of this, a fully documented leaflet has been issued by ATV. Apply, on a postcard please, to the address at bottom left.

BOOK COMMERCIALS IN THE SAME TIME SEGMENTS AS THESE GREAT ATV FAVOURITES

Most of these popular programmes appear regularly among TAM-rating's weekly "Top Ten."

LONDON	Number of households viewing
Sunday Night at the London Palladium	660,000
I Love Lucy	660,000
Jack Jackson Show	560,000
Robin Hood	550,000
Roy Rogers	500,000
MIDLANDS	
Hit the Limit	330,000
Cross Current	324,000
Superman	291,000
Gun Law	285,000
Robin Hood	285,000

These average audience figures are based on known ratings for the above programmes applied to the audiences that it is anticipated will be achieved by next autumn. The figures represent households, not viewers, so that commercials in most of these programmes will actually be seen by over 1½ million people in London and by over 1 million in the Midlands.

Visco-Static oil instead of ordinary oil the wear on piston rings would be reduced by 80%. Visco-Static oil was further said to reduce engine wear and at least to double the life of an engine in good condition. The ITA found that the 80% saving in piston wear could not be extended to cylinder wear to the degree claimed for it and prevailed on the company to modify its commercials, retaining only the 80% saving on piston rings.

A jubilant Donald Chapman said afterwards, 'The gratifying thing is that as a result of these three cases and the pressure of the last three months on all these matters, our screens have been largely cleaned up as far as extravagance of claims is concerned.'

Nonetheless, in 1959 Domestos – the household bleach – claimed, 'Domestos kills all known germs in one hour.'

It wasn't till 1964, when the ITCA – Independent Television Companies Association – set up a committee to vet commercial scripts before they went out to programme companies, that commercial claims came under any

Gumption never has it so good.

Can the Man-with-the-Gong
send YOUR sales mounting?

CINEMA ADVERTISING catches the consumer in a relaxed and receptive mood. The pill of persuasion, sweetened by the jam of entertainment, goes down easily. That is why so many astute advertisers pin their faith to this form of publicity, and in particular to the Man-with-the-Gong—symbolising The Rank Organisation—as a past (and present!) master in the production and exhibition of screen advertising. He has the experience and the equipment, the techniques and the stars; he has, too, busy cinemas in which the messages of advertisers are carried to an immense and responsive public through filmlets, two-minute films and the monthly magazine-films "Tips" and (very shortly now) "Shop".

Isn't it more than likely that the Man-with-the-Gong can give your sales a lift? Put the subject down on the agenda for your next conference.

All the Rank screen advertising activities for Great Britain and Overseas are centred in **J. Arthur Rank Screen Services Limited,** 11 Hill Street, London, W.1. (Grosvenor 6353).

rigorous control. Before that, programme companies used their discretion on scripts and, having other priorities, did not always apply the necessary firmness. Viewed today, many of those early commercials were filled with such a spirit of honest endeavour and enthusiasm for the product that it seems almost churlish to call their claims misleading.

There were some advertisers, however, who carried enthusiasm for their products to the point of investing them with properties that were not quite what they seemed. Dental and medical items were especially prone to boosting their images with impressively clinical ingredients. In 1959 the dental profession erupted after several years of standing by while certain substances were claimed to be of specific benefit to teeth and gums. The British Dental Association protested at last, and the ITA, having investigated, announced that the commercials concerned would be withdrawn or modified. The role of toothpaste advertising on television was and is, however, recognized by dental experts as being responsible for fostering awareness about dental hygiene. Only six out of ten households possessed a toothbrush in 1959.

Commercials took another knock in 1959 when the expression 'subliminal advertising' became part of the language. It stemmed from findings in the USA that some advertisers there were using this psychological technique in television commercials. To all appearances, these ads were no different from the rest of the television advertising output, but in fact each contained a message in addition to the apparent one. This secondary message was incorporated within the commercial but displayed on screen for a fractional amount of time, enough for it to be picked up just below the level of consciousness – a level at which the mind had a more powerful sense of recall, and was more vulnerable to persuasion. The phenomenon became the subject of a great deal of public debate and was genuinely feared. The ITA responded with firm assurances that subliminality would never happen here, although how any conscious testing for an 'unconscious' or 'subconscious' agent could be arranged is difficult to imagine.

1959 was also the year which led to the marketing of the 'blab-off'.

Commercials were suddenly too loud. Readers wrote to the press in droves complaining about the change in volume when the commercials appeared. People became convinced that the programme companies deliberately altered the sound balance during breaks. Experts put their views. One professor of medicine claimed that commercials that were too loud could harm his patients, and went so far as to post nurses by the volume control of the television set at his hospital, ready to adjust it before and after every commercial break. But the programme companies denied any suggestion that this was a scheme to get people to pay attention to the commercials.

Opposite: This trade press ad in January 1956 was part of a long campaign designed to remind advertisers that television was not the only moving picture medium. The 'Man-with-the-Gong' put up a well-reasoned fight.

Meanwhile, some enterprising manufacturer hit out at the advertisers with a new, lethal weapon – the blab-off – which was effective within armchair's range of the television set. The viewers could sit with a blab-off at the ready and cut out the sound without moving a step. The blab-off created tremendous interest at the 1960 Radio Show where its powers were demonstrated, and at $2\frac{1}{2}$ guineas there were plenty of purchasers.

The pattern of press correspondence altered with the availability of a blab-off. Now for every bunch of complaining letters, there were always a few who wrote in to say that since they had this marvellous invention they did not have to bother getting up to turn the volume down, and that watching television was a positive pleasure without those noisy commercials.

In November 1959, *Daily Herald* television writer Philip Philips was moved to declare, 'I shall now stop arguing about whether viewers dislike TV commercials or not. I know. They don't dislike them: they *loathe* them.' He printed a selection of anti-commercial letters from his postbag, including one from a lady reader in Lancashire. 'There are too many commercials. Ask any woman. She hardly ever sees them. The commercial is her cue to fill the hot-water bottles, cut sandwiches, fetch the coal.'

Perhaps this letter reveals far more about the status of many women in 1959 than their antagonism towards commercials, but the anonymous writer from Lancashire did pinpoint one major complaint. There were too many commercials, for manufacturers, having found that television advertising led to dramatic upswings in sales, were only too keen to buy every available second.

But with all that 1959 had brought in the way of anti-commercial television feeling, the viewing figures reflected an entirely different opinion. Independent Television still maintained its sizeable lead over the BBC.

The teething infant could well afford a measure of disgruntlement.

PART 6

'Forever Blowing Bubbles'
Washing Powder Ads Infinitum

T'was on a Monday morning
When I beheld my darling,
She looked so neat and charming
In every high degree,
She looked so neat and nimble oh,
A washing out the linen oh,
Dashing away with a smoothing iron,
Dashing away with a smoothing iron,
Dashing away with a smoothing iron,
She stole my heart away.

T'was on a Tuesday morning . . .
A hanging out the linen oh . . .

T'was on a Wednesday morning . . .
A bringing in the linen oh . . .

T'was on a Thursday morning . . .
Ironing of the linen oh . . .

T'was on a Friday morning . . .
A folding of the linen oh . . .

T'was on a Saturday morning . . .
An airing of the linen oh . . .

T'was on a Sunday morning . . .
A wearing of the linen oh . . .
Dashing away, etc . . .

(mid-nineteenth century Somerset folk
song collected by Cecil Sharp)

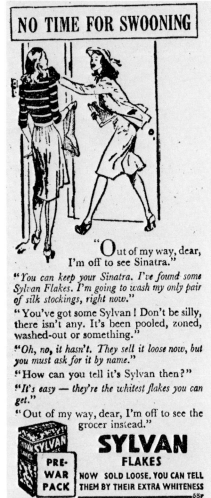

1944 newspaper ad. A glimpse of long-gone priorities.

In November 1955 the *Sunday Dispatch* published the results of a readers' opinion poll of their favourite commercials. The top three were: Murraymints, Shell and Guinness; then followed Freeman Hardy & Willis (shoeshops), Mortons peas, Norvic shoes, Omo, Oxo, Surf and Watneys ale.

The big surprise in this early, therefore limited, poll is that two of the top ten products were household detergents. Today a similar poll would certainly never include a detergent commercial. The genre is, and has been for many years, almost universally unpopular, and yet detergent manufacturers remain consistently in the top-spender league in TV commercial expenditure. In fact, the very first list (published in March 1956) of the top spenders on television included some familiar names. Omo came second in the list with a total expenditure of £69,405; Surf fourth with £67,777; Persil tenth with £36,511; Daz twelfth with £35, 237; and Tide seventeenth with £32,430.

But before commercial television stands accused of having brought about this vast spending on a commodity that is a necessary purchase, it would be as well to take account of a House of Commons debate which was charged with passion, politics and laughter. It took place on 9 February 1954.

Sir Richard Acland asked leave of the Commons to introduce the Price Control (No. 1) Bill to reduce the retail price of Surf, Daz, Fab, Persil, Tide and other soap powders, soap substitutes and detergents. The report from *The Times* of 10 February 1954 continues:

> . . . he said that this was the first of what he hoped would be a series of useful and popular measures, all designed to reduce the cost of living (*Opposition cheers*). Amid further cheers he produced empty flattened soap powder packets to illustrate the purport of the Bill, announcing the proposed price reduction for each product. Those retailed at 1/11d were to be reduced to 1/7d and those which were 1/- were to be 10d under the Bill. He said that on many packets there was a 'money-saving coupon' for the purchase of a large packet of detergent. In this connexion the word 'large' was a trade term meaning 'small' (*laughter*).
>
> Members of Parliament now had a right and duty to tell the big noises of privately-owned big business to stop playing the fool with public money, to cut down advertising to reasonable proportions, and reduce prices (*Opposition cheers*). Money spent on advertising was public money. When, for example, D. H. Evans displayed a picture of a smug polar bear enjoying himself with a rather scantily dressed lady, the taxpayers were paying for one half of the show. (An Hon. Member: 'Which half?' – *laughter*). It was wrong that the playboys of the big business world should now, by their advertising antics, stand in the way of the housewife, who might otherwise get things more cheaply (*Opposition cheers*).
>
> Mr Harmar Nicholls (Peterborough, C.) opposed the Bill. He said he could not tell whether Sir Richard Acland had been introducing a Bill or making a mock auction.

A still from the 1960 Wirl commercial, a Ziegfeld-style production which was to become a folly.

Someone's mum did use Persil in this 1960 commercial.

When Brigadier Clarke (Portsmouth West, C.) asked 'How much was he paid?' Mr Arthur Lewis objected and the Speaker directed that the remark should be withdrawn.

Brigadier Clarke: 'I willingly withdraw that remark, but I thought that was the best bit of advertising I had heard for detergents (*laughter*).'

Leave was granted, and the Bill was brought in and read a first time.

The fate of the Price Control (No. 1) Bill was cruel. It did not survive its second reading.

There were several washing powder companies in the mid-fifties – all identified with different brand names. Thomas Hedley, Hudson & Knight, Lever Brothers and Procter & Gamble traded under their respective names, but their products were, in fact, manufactured by either Lever Brothers or Procter & Gamble. Thomas Hedley was actually owned by Procter & Gamble, and Lever Brothers had acquired Hudson & Knight. Crosfields, the original Persil manufacturers, had been bought out by Lever Brothers some years previously.

The washing of clothes was at that time a necessary, time-consuming and fatiguing process. If the household lacked a permanent hot-water supply, and most did, water had first to be heated, and when this was ready the clothes had to be washed using either bars of household soap (like Fairy or Sunlight), soap powder or soap flakes. Often a combination of the two was used; the bar soap was applied for scrubbing heavy stains and then there was a further wash in soap powder. White clothes and linen had to be bleached, and since the whole washing process was done by hand in the great majority of households – washing machines had no mass market – the weekly wash could take a whole day, even allowing for decent weather for drying. The ironing and putting away took up the best part of another day, and in wet weather the household, usually equipped with a 'pulley' for this contingency, could spend the best part of a week amid washing in various stages of getting dry.

Washing, of all household activities, impinged most on the domestic scene and presented a tremendous burden to the person responsible for it, in most cases the woman of the house. Laundries were available for the better off, and were used for household linen far more generally than today.

What the two big manufacturers had to offer was something new in washing powders – detergents – which had grease-dissolving as well as soap content and were presented like laundering Sir Galahads come to free the housewife from wash-day tyranny. (Ajax scouring powder later realized this metaphor by using a White Knight in one campaign.) When commercial television came along, all four rushed to the screen with their wares, competing for attention while selling what appeared to be the same commodity.

Persil, which had been on the market since 1909, had a long history of 'Someone's mum isn't using Persil' campaigns in the press and on posters, showing two little girls in identical dresses – one white and the other off-white. Persil carried this theme into their early commercials along with a bright and quite charming jingle.

Someone's mum just doesn't know
What someone's mum really ought to know,
So someone's mum better get to know
That Persil washes whiter, whiter,
Persil washes whiter.

The 1960 Omo girl

The appeal was very much in the Persil tradition – an extension of their pre-TV image. Persil also had the advantage of being a brand name with a long and trusted history.

Right from the start, Surf used one of the most imaginative concepts in the history of television advertising. It overcame the problem of showing someone actually doing the washing, but nevertheless drew attention to the whiteness of the wash and also, remarkably, put a man in an inferior position to a woman while involving him in many familiar domestic situations. This was achieved by creating a 'character' called Mrs Bradshaw who never appeared on the screen, though her presence was real enough – communicated to the viewer through the character who did appear, Mrs Bradshaw's lodger. He would address the camera on the subject of Mrs Bradshaw, and at one point would always draw attention to the newly-done pile of washing she had just brought in, then take an item over to the window saying, 'Hold it up to the light, not a stain and shining bright.' The lodger was often landed with Mrs Bradshaw's 'cousin Nelly's nipper' to look after, and in assuming this or any other typically 'female' domestic role he reacted with spontaneous goodwill and in no sense made capital in the way that has become a stereotype of being 'domestic'. He was under Mrs Bradshaw's thumb but not to the extent of making her a figure of fun. The lodger was quite often on the receiving end of Mrs Bradshaw's anger but always because he deserved it.

Above all, the series broke many of the unwritten rules. It made an ordinary working man an entirely credible person. He had an ordinary speaking voice, and in an area of commercials that has always featured women as secondary to the product and usually doing little more than react to the claims and later evidence for them presented by a man, it still stands unique.

The early Omo commercials were animated – very appealing – and so were safe from the perils of comparison tests and piles of washing. After the first few years Omo featured a little girl in a white dress running along a wall with what became known as the 'Omo tune' in the background – an instrumental composed by Cliff Adams which perfectly caught the hesitant/confident manner of the child. The style of this commercial was something of a breakthrough, because it was a complete match of music to film and a very soft sell. A *Daily Mail* poll of its readers in 1962 on their favourite commercials pulled in most votes for Omo.

Persil, Surf and Omo are all products of Lever Brothers, whose style of TV advertising has remained throughout twenty-five years popular or, at least, less annoying.

Tide was another matter. From the outset its television appearances were brash, noisy and full of gimmicks like the White Tide Man in his pristine suit and the booming voiceover – 'Get your clothes clean. Not only clean but deep-down clean. Tide clean.'

Daz pioneered the Brand X method of selling. The early days of Brand X did produce some classic pieces of film when some of the women who had their washing done in Daz and Brand X, unaccustomed to a visit from a man with a microphone, television cameras and crew, and being unversed, through lack of a television set, in the expected responses, just chattered on as if to a neighbour while the unnerved presenter would politely strain to get their attention back to the washing line. But by 1961 the Brand X technique had moved the Independent Television Authority to action, and it announced in March of that year that comparative claims that were presented factually in detergent and soap powder advertising would not be allowed in future. Instead, said the ITA, 'simple, conventional uses of comparatives or superlatives' would be allowed, but no other words which could be taken to mean that the claims were universally valid. Comparisons in filmed demonstrations would also be excluded. The ITA went on to express the hope that the measures would 'take into account the marginal nature of the differences between many of the products of this highly competitive industry. The great variety of conditions in which products are used in the home makes conclusive substantiation of claims of supremacy of one product over others almost impossible.'

Thomas Hedley, who numbered Daz and Tide among their products,

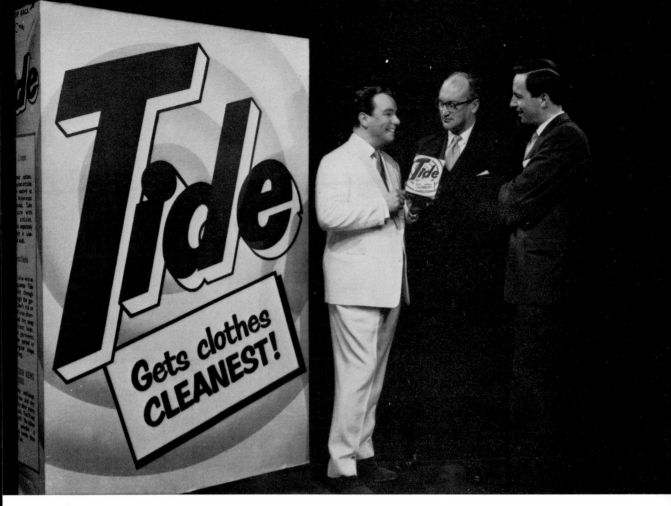

Above: The White Tide Man – actor Ronnie Blythe on set at Rediffusion.

Left: An early-Sixties Tide commercial on the line 'The Bluinite Tide for the white that catches the eye'.

Below: Another variation of the Tide copyline was the white Tide that catches the eye.

Above left: 1957 animated ad for Persil

Above centre: A Persil mum in 1961, one of the first in the 'What is a mum?' campaign.

defended comparative advertising in a statement issued shortly after the ITA announcement. The company said that it was not enough for the advertiser to be allowed to describe his product to the consumer. He must also be allowed to describe its merits relative to other available products.

At the end of a very long statement pointing out the advantages of proving by comparison their product was honestly the best, therefore a vital stimulus to the production of new and improved products, Hedley stated:

> This is of absolutely vital importance in a market such as this, where the competing products are purchased on average weekly by sixteen million housewives. In such a market no manufacturer can hope to sell an unsatisfactory product more than once. The growth of his business, and in turn the maintenance of product variety and of constant product improvement, depends on competitive yet truthful exposition of his products' benefits and valid superiorities.

Hedley concluded by saying that the subject of television advertising should not be considered in a vacuum but as one feature of the intricate fabric of our national economy, the essence of which is competition. But the argument did not convince the ITA, who went ahead and amended the rules. And a Lancashire shopowner announced his plans to put a washing powder named Brand X on the market.

This late fifties/early sixties period of intensive detergent and soap powder marketing was known as the 'soap war', of which some battle trophies may still be around. It was the time of the great giveaway, when plastic flowers

were enough of a novelty to be accepted free along with the washing powder. Roses and daffodils predominated, while the Fairy Snowman went around giving out cash prizes. More practical shoppers took advantage of free plastic mixing bowls (many, to their credit, still in use), but the cumulative effect of so much of this kind of advertising eventually antagonized even the most tolerant viewers, and disenchantment with commercials in general set in. Perhaps because of the general fuss about commercials, or possibly because the market was not ready for it, the impact of a brand-new washing product – launched at vast expense by Hudson & Knight in 1960 and called Wirl – fell completely flat. Where Wirl departed from other washing powder commercials was in making a central feature of washing machines. The commercial showed a street lined on either side with washing machines; behind each was a very pretty 'housewife' who leaned forward over the machine holding a packet of Wirl. It represented the shape of things to come, the inevitable follow-on to the revolution in washing powders – the wholesale acceptance of the washing machine. No one, though, took much notice.

1957 saw the launch of Fairy Snow – the last soap powder on the British market. Fairy Snow claimed to give 'Washday white without washday red', an obvious dig at detergents which had been rumoured to cause skin rashes. Fairy Snow's most memorable campaign came later, and featured popular husband and wife entertainers Joan and Leslie Randall. This format established Fairy Snow, with its friendly banter rooted in the fabric of a happy marriage.

Betty Driver, a notable comedienne (who was later to achieve global fame for her role as Betty Turpin in the serial 'Coronation Street', which was then a mere three years old), was used in a campaign for Oxydol showing the power of its whitening abilities because North Country air was dirtier than the South's. Oxydol was withdrawn in 1973 after forty-two years on the market.

Omo decided on a change of tactics in 1963, as it was launching new Omo with WM 7. Competition was hotting up and the campaign needed a very special presenter, someone with total impact. The search for someone with the right qualities covered all the options, and among those testing for the part – which included a man with one arm and a man who wore an eye-patch – was a young man from Australia. Test commercials were made of the seventeen final candidates and were watched by sample audiences whose preferences were noted. The young man from Australia had not rated too highly among the professionals, but the results showed an overwhelming vote in his favour. So a jubilant Alan Freeman arrived on a scooter – clutching a bottle of wine – to sign the Omo contract.

The commercial film production company then embarked on a laundry safari of the Welsh valleys and coalfields, where they hired cars and drove round offering to do people's washing. The film producer himself did two lots of washing, all in an effort to demonstrate that Omo added brightness to cleanness and whiteness. Omo also added Bright, bright, brightness.

Variations on whiteness, cleanness, brightness, so clean you can see the difference, cleanest clean you've ever seen, shining shining white, had been mainly forced on the advertisers by the earlier ITA ban on comparative advertising. But Persil kept very much to its 'mother' appeal, and in 1964 Mai Zetterling directed a series of commercials for the product on the theme of 'What is a mum?' that had great emotional effect.

The 'caring' aspect of Persil spread, and although the introduction of colour television in 1969 brought prettier pictures it brought almost nothing in the way of an innovative approach to the formula for selling washing powder. In fact, almost the reverse was true when the 'window test' was brought back for the 1979 launch of Daz Automatic washing powder.

One innovation that was very quickly given the thumbs-down during the marketing from 1968 onwards of 'biological' powders was the word 'understains'. Coined for Omo Biological to epitomize the ultimate in human residue on clothing, the word seemed to strike at the very heart of human frailty; it was universally objected to and finally crept away into silence.

Bibby Food Products of Liverpool had virtual monopoly in the automatic powder market until the launch of Persil Automatic in 1968, when there were comparatively few owners of automatic machines. The Bibby product,

Mrs Bradshaw's lodger – otherwise, actor John Warren.

PAT, had a loyal band of users for whom shopkeepers always kept a stock. Persil Automatic arrived with a flourish and was prominently displayed on supermarket shelves, where the magic of the Persil name gave the product a head start. Bibby fought back with a national television campaign urging shoppers to ask for PAT if they didn't see it on display at their grocery store. A leading supermarket executive called the move 'a desperate measure', but Bibby's campaign attracted a lot of attention and led to an increase in sales for a time. However, PAT eventually collapsed under the avalanche of automatic brands that followed through the seventies in Persil's wake.

The 'soap' business wore out its welcome with commercial watchers a long time ago and the question that is always asked of the industry is, 'Why the incessant advertising?' The industry is highly competitive although, as stated, the many brands on the market are manufactured by just two main companies – Procter & Gamble (Ariel, Bold, Daz, Dreft, Fairy Snow, and Tide) and Lever Brothers (Omo, Persil, Radiant and Surf). Research and development play as big a part in the manufacture of washing powders as in any other manufacturing industry, even though one soap powder looks very like another, but having improved a product it must also be sold heavily enough to make it profitable.

Washing powder commercials have, until recently, stuck firmly to selling the product on its own merits rather than around an image. The two major companies have approached their markets in distinctly different ways. Procter & Gamble, an American firm, seems to care less for 'sympathetic' advertising than going straight out there, making a noise and selling –

whereas Lever Brothers have opted for a more affectionate angle.

One major exception was the gentle marketing of Fairy Liquid for the washing of dishes, which has concentrated on the mother/child relationship to emphasize the importance of soft hands. The role of washing-up liquid cannot be overstressed in its contribution to improving a task that prior to its appearance was much less pleasant.

Strangely, despite public antipathy to P & G's other commercials and the contrasting preference for Lever Brothers (in comparison studies), the P & G message comes through much more memorably. P & G are therefore in no hurry to change a winning formula.

Without commercial television, the progress of the soap manufacturing industry would have had, according to some, a far slower rate of development. It is also doubtful whether the ownership of washing machines would have been so widespread, as without mass purchase the price would have remained much higher.

Incidentally, it is interesting that since the beginning of commercial radio in 1973 no washing powder manufacturer has used that medium for advertising.

During the course of Independent Television the soap industry has reached advertising saturation point on several occasions and has had to ease up by ITA/IBA regulation or by mutual agreement between the two manufacturers. No other product has been through such peaks and troughs. Without advertising, and left to people to decide for themselves, many sectors of the industry would almost certainly have failed.

PART 7

'The Folks Who Live on the Chill'
Frozen Food Pioneers

Peas, green, boiled

INGREDIENTS – Green peas, mint, butter, salt and pepper.

METHOD – Shell the peas, put them into boiling water, add a little salt and sprig of mint, and boil, with the saucepan uncovered, from 10 to 25 minutes, according to age and variety. Drain well, put them into a hot vegetable dish, season with pepper, add a small piece of butter, and serve.

TIME – From 10 to 25 minutes. Cost, from 6d per peck.

SEASONABLE – from May to September.

(from *Mrs Beeton's Cookery Book*)

There really was a Mr Birdseye – Clarence Birdseye – an American who bought out a company called Instant Postum in 1928 and formed General Foods – which was in turn bought by Unilever just after the Second World War.

In 1946 the Ministry of Food gave Birdseye permission to go into production because the company was willing to freeze herring – a vital product at the time because of the fishing industry. Later this licence was extended to peas, which they manufactured with severely limited production facilities from a factory that had no roof but a tarpaulin – a sitting target for thunderstorms, and very uncomfortable to work in. The firm started advertising their frozen blackcurrants in 1947, both in the press and with point-of-sale on grocers' counters. This first year's advertising cost them around £500.

In the early fifties, when there was still food rationing, Birdseye froze peaches and pineapple for the fruit-deprived home market, but this operation failed when canned fruit came on to the scene.

When commercial television was on the horizon, Birdseye decided to use the medium from the start in order to reach as wide a market as possible. This was at a time when fridges were regarded as beyond the reach of most incomes and a glimpse of one in an American movie was the closest most people got. Therefore the emphasis in the commercials was on convenience, taste and price.

The first-ever Birdseye commercial, which was also the first for any frozen product, was for sliced green beans, and showed a pretty woman wearing an apron standing somewhat self-consciously by a cooker in a disarmingly artificial garden setting. The female voiceover spoke in studied Queen's English.

> If you could cook your beans in the garden they would be the freshest in the world. And that's how fresh they are all the year round when you buy Birdseye quick-frozen sliced green beans. Quick-freezing seals in the natural goodness and flavour. The 2/- carton serves four and there's also a small size – enough for two. A wide choice, real value, quick-frozen freshness.
>
> That's Birdseye.

This idea of cooking on location to convey freshness was extended to their commercial for fish, an identiscript commercial with the relevant words substituted for the product. And viewers by now would have become aware of the curious fanfare that introduced every Birdseye commercial of that period.

Fish fingers, destined to become the *sine qua non* of children's cuisine, were launched in a very matter-of-fact way – using the same female voiceover, which was now losing its 'reading aloud' tone of voice:

> Here's the very latest way of getting a quick nourishing meal – Birdseye quick-frozen fish fingers. They're all fish with that wonderful (*pause*) sea fresh flavour captured by quick-freezing (*very rushed to compensate for the pause*).
>
> Children love fish fingers. There are no bones and they're already cooked and crumbed. Just heat them. Six fish fingers cost only 1/8d and they're plenty for two. They're delicious.

Anyone who remembers the scene in the film *East of Eden* where James Dean looks helplessly at the train-load of waterlogged lettuce which he had helped to pack and freeze, must feel a shiver at the gamble Birdseye took in launching one frozen product after another when the only trading outlets were relatively few small grocery shops sufficiently persuaded to spare the freezer space. In 1956 the number of such shops was a mere 23,000 (there were no supermarkets) and this was putting a brake on Birdseye's business. To popularize those shops and convince others to go over to freezers (along

with their normal stock), the 'Stop at the Birdseye Shop' campaign was begun. Birdseye shops were identified by a prominent door label featuring the Birdseye bird. These commercials featured a jingle with a catchy tune and lyrics which made the point, and made it, and made it.

Captain Birdseye makes his first appearance.

> Stop at the Birdseye shop,
> Stop at the Birdseye shop,
> Stop at the Birdseye,
> Shop at the Birdseye,
> Stop at the Birdseye shop.

This campaign paid enormous dividends. By 1965 the number of Birdseye shops had increased to 125,000. And with the growth in frozen food sales, came the inevitable spin-off, the mass marketing of fridges with freezing compartments and, eventually, freezers. The arrival of supermarkets and, later, freezer centres owed a great deal to Birdseye's faith in commercial television, the only medium that could reach the mass market it hoped to capture.

Alan Parker directing
Ben (Darren Cockerill
from Leeds) in his first
Beefburger commercial.
Leaning over is Neil
Godfrey, who created the
campaign. This first film
was shown in 1973.

FACING PAGE:
Top: Mary, played by
Heather McDonald, sees
Ben for the first time.

Below: The last goodbye.

The availability of frozen food has given women especially a measure of freedom from everyday cooking and taken the pressure off those who work and have limited time for shopping.

Birdseye's early television advertising highlighted the practicality of the products and seldom strayed into whimsy (apart from presentational aspects like the Birdseye Room, from which the presenter would introduce the product and often show a meal being cooked from beginning to end during the commercial). An exception in 1967 was Captain Birdseye, played by Canadian actor John Hewer. There were doubts in the advertising profession about Captain Birdseye's pulling power, but he continued until 1971 when he was dropped from the fish fingers campaigns. This earned him an obituary in *The Times*, the only occasion when a commercial character has been afforded such an honour. In 1974 he returned in full colour.

Another campaign that attracted much attention showed the 'Cannonball pea', which was too hard to be allowed into the pack with the tender Birdseye peas. This aroused great public sympathy, and Birdseye often had to answer

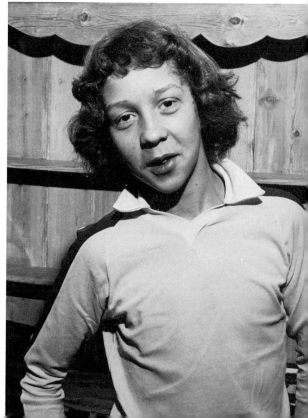

June Whitfield as
Shakespeare's wife.

Pinocchio's mum – June
Whitfield again.

letters from the public about an animated vegetable.

One early commercial claim for peas – 'fresh as the moment they were picked' – is strongly echoed in the 'Birdseye peas, sweet as the moment when the pod went pop' jingle composed by Steve Race, which has accompanied four cheek-popping little girls to date.

The popularity of all these was as nothing compared to the hold which the campaign begun in 1974 for Beefburgers took on television viewers. Filmed by Alan Parker (later to direct *Midnight Express* for the cinema) it starred three children – Ben, Dan and Mary. There were some complaining letters at first about the children's northern accents, but these were short-lived as the three caught the imagination. Dan left the series, and Ben and Mary continued a very real relationship based on her obvious love for him and his not quite returning this to her. Would they ever be more than friends? The brilliant direction, drawing star performances from the children, the lighting and the camerawork brought the satisfaction of a film experience to under a minute of time.

A late-Fifties commercial for Eskimo Frozen Food Ltd. Advertising frozen peas, its copyline was 'Eskimo frozen sunshine peas – picked at their sunsweet best'. Not only a tongue-twister but also a sublime mixture of metaphors. 'Sweet as the moment when the pod went pop' (Birdseye's pea slogan) used the same elements as the Eskimo line but made them work.

After the inevitable parting – Ben's parents were moving to Australia – Birdseye were beseeched in letters not to let him go. Didn't they realize, people wrote, that it would break Mary's heart? One teen magazine editor wrote to the company about having run a feature on Ben some time before, and hearing he was to be written out she had printed a coupon for readers to return if they felt strongly that Ben should be brought back. There were 432 replies and a couple of petitions, which were being passed on to Birdseye with the request that the company print some sort of reply or explanation as the editor thought many people would genuinely miss him.

Since Ben's departure Mary has reappeared in company with twin boys, her new neighbours. Now, very much the little mother, she calls to mind an earlier Birdseye message about watching 'them grow and grow'. That was for fish fingers. But Mary gives every reason to suppose that beefburgers have the same effect.

PART 8

'Small Fry'

Admags 1955–63

From the giants of television advertising to the ones who would have grown if given the chance. From the full-page display ad to the classified columns. From the hypermarket to the cornershop. There was a time when television advertising was open to those who could not or chose not to afford the expensive individual spot.

In the Parliamentary debates of the mid fifties, the subject of 'shoppers' guides' and 'advertising documentaries' had caused some apprehension amongst a group of Labour MPs. The ITA Act had made provision for this form of advertising and put it into practice almost as soon as the first programme companies opened. These programmes, lasting around fifteen minutes each, were the 'advertising magazines' better known as 'admags'.

The admag was unique to Britain, and there was a kind of backdoor bravado about them in the way every admag transmission cheekily bumped up the amount of advertising per clock hour. But the viewers never complained. They loved the quaint little programmes, which provided the same fascination as flipping through a mail-order catalogue. There was no telling what would come next.

The presenters of admags, some already popular personalities, some unknowns, soon had a big public following and became like family friends.

The format for admags was somewhat limited, since it had to take place in a setting appropriate to the demonstration and display of the advertisers' products, leaving everything in easy reach of the presenter. Depending on how many seconds the advertiser had paid for (the rate per minute was around £400) the product would be on show – the average length of time was between fifteen and twenty seconds.

With this in mind, ABC-TV's first admag was a very ambitious production indeed. Called 'Elizabeth Allan Goes Shopping' it went out to the London area and featured Elizabeth Allan (well known to most people through her frequent appearances on BBC television) doing the rounds of one London store per show. The stores were very upmarket – Harrods, Marshall & Snelgrove, etc. – and entirely suited Miss Allan's 'countess' manner. The accent was on quality at a reasonable price and it was done with great style.

Apart from a few exceptions, such as Katie Boyle and Muriel Young, most

admag presenters were much more homely and ordinary – like trusted aunts and uncles. The department store location gave way to simplicity and ease of presentation. Doris Rogers ('What's in Store'), for example, faced the camera from behind a desk. A shop set was simple and appropriate, hence 'Shop in the South' with Sylvia Peters and Macdonald Hobley (both BBC personalities); 'Shop on the Corner' with Donald Bisset; 'Watson's Store' with Jack Howarth (another to become such a success in 'Coronation Street') and Vi Stevens, which was shown in the Midlands and North; and 'In Store', which had a star cast of Kenneth Horne, Richard Murdoch and Tommy Trinder. Fanny and Johnnie Cradock presented cookery admags, as did Philip Harben and Marguerite Patten.

'Flair' was a programme of young fashions. It had a reputation for class since it was arranged by top fifties fashion photographer John French. Less formal was 'Girl with a Date', another admag aimed at the younger market.

When it finished in 1957 Peter Black, the eminent television critic, expressed disappointment. 'The programmes are often as hilarious as instructive,' he wrote. 'Girl with a Date' ended because the producer had suffered too much from the advertisers. He explained to Black that the pressure from them to make the dialogue more and more ecstatic over their products had become too much. 'They just can't have enough ecstacy,' he said.

Scripts for admags were the responsibility of the programme company, who would first of all hold a briefing conference with the advertisers' representatives, the ad agency representatives, the programme director, the writer and the company's head of admags. After information on the products and possible presentation had been discussed, the company would present the advertisers and their retinue with a draft script for their consideration. The bargaining would then begin, because each advertiser believed in his product to the exclusion of all others and would take it in turn to explain to the writer his particular case.

When it was time for the telerecording, admags went out live, and the advertisers would return with their team to watch the programme being made. Bolstered by the importance of being part of television and with so much hinging on the way their goods were shown, they would at this stage press for the maximum close-up for their packshot (the picture of their pack) or demonstration. This did not always have the desired effect.

Remembering his admag days one director recalled the occasion when he had to film a chunk of Spam dressed with mayonnaise. The Spam representative demanded closer and closer shots of the Spam until the director felt he was right into the pores of this lump of meat. At that moment a bluebottle landed on the mayonnaise and, because of the magnification, appeared on the television screens like some grotesque monster.

Another over-zealous advertiser ruined the magazine for all the participants when he got edgy about the way his company's shoes were being shown. He kept insisting they were 'pointing the wrong way' and finally could take it no longer, even after the shoes had been repositioned several times. In desperation he burst on to the set shouting, 'I'll do it myself,' at which the whole telerecording had to be abandoned, ruining a week's work.

His anxiety could be understood, as most products had little more than ten seconds to make their impact. But the pressure on the directors could become even more severe, knowing their every move was being watched and judged by people whose sum of knowledge about television seemed to consist of the words 'close-up'. One director, who confesses he had nearly had enough of this untutored direction, used to answer the request for further close-ups by pretending to swing the lens to close-up but only actually swinging the hood

to the same lens as before, saying, 'Is that better?' The placated advertiser would almost always agree that it was.

These tactics relieved the strain for a short time, but this man's final bow from admags was made the day he was asked to inject 'some movement' into a fifteen-minute admag for one difficult customer. The customer got movement – for the whole fifteen minutes, when the camera simply tracked forwards and backwards the whole time. The effect on the screen was like being in a bad swell at sea.

Sometimes the actors suffered. One was called upon to say, 'Try this beer,' take a mouthful and continue, 'It's delicious.' The unfortunate man tried at rehearsal and nearly spat it out, then on recording he managed to take a mouthful but pulled such a face in doing it that the advertiser was given a free spot in a later programme to placate him.

Tommy Trinder, a lifetime non-smoker, was rendered almost speechless

Fanny and Johnny Cradock and an upmarket admag production.

'Jim's Inn', the greatest admag of them all. *Left to right*: Jack Edwardes, Jimmy Hanley, Maggie Hanley, Victor Platt (with dog) John Sherlock, a stand-in, Roma Cresswell and two locals.

by a cigarette he was forced to smoke and appear to enjoy.

The greatest of all the admags, because it became a programme which was followed as closely as 'Coronation Street' is today, was 'Jim's Inn'. The action took place in a pub, and the cast was headed by the late Jimmy Hanley.

The classic tribute to the selling power of 'Jim's Inn' was the account of the fur coat sale at 'Jones and Higgins of Peckham'. There were to be just fifty coats in the sale, and the presentation problem – how to convey all this information in fifteen seconds – seemed very difficult. The solution was for Roma (who ran the local beauty salon) to throw open the door of the pub while the four male characters gave a low whistle. Maggie (Hanley) then said, 'What a lovely coat! Where did you get it?' 'Jones and Higgins of Peckham, they've got a sale on. It was reduced from £70 to £50,' replied Roma within the alloted timespan, to everyone's relief. Next morning the department store was virtually under siege, the queue headed by a North London woman clutching five ten-pound notes.

One distinguished actor, John Carson, played a local spic in 'Jim's Inn'. His job was to flash a packet of Player's cigarettes and say, 'Have one of these. It's the tobacco that counts.' For the part he had to look slightly seedy and use an accent to match. One day after the show, there was a small party during which an executive from Player's was introduced to him. The Player's man took one

Rediffusion director Pat Baker with admag presenter the Duke of Bedford.

look at the spiv and, in a voice redolent of all the right places, said, 'Oh, you're the chap who does the Player's. I think we had better give you Weights to do.' Carson accepted the downgrading. But a few years later when he had started to do some voiceover work, he was approached by Player's again, this time to sign an exclusive contract for their use of his voice on a series of Player's commercials.

'Jim's Inn' gained such increasing popularity that an LP record was produced for fans of the programme. Called 'Singalong at Jim's Inn', it featured the whole cast singing old-time favourites – excluding cuts from comedy shows, this is the only record of its kind in TV history.

The admag format widened to include specialist subjects like holidays, cars and do-it-yourself, while Marks and Spencer took fifteen-minute admags to advertise their range.

A number of comedy admags appeared at the end of the fifties. Comedienne/impressionist Janet Brown and her husband Peter Butterworth starred in 'For Pete's Sake', a twenty-minute programme in which the couple would parody well-known films with the help of a regular company of players – including the show's scriptwriters. A typical episode of 'For Pete's Sake' would open with Janet and Peter sitting in front of a TV set. One of them would mention having seen a certain film and be asked, 'What did you

Wistful Valerie Singleton on set.

remember?' At this the picture would fade into the screen and the cast would enact some film parody. Scriptwriter Brad Ashton remembered being one of a pair of bearded prisoners in a version of *The Count of Monte Cristo.* The scene showed him discussing with his similarly bearded cellmate the possibility of escape. His companion, however, insisted pessimistically that they wouldn't get away with it because of their beards. This enabled Ashton to reply, 'Don't worry, I've got something that will get rid of them. Look what I've smuggled in, it's a Telefunken cordless electric razor.' This Telefunken advertisement drew 5,000 replies, which knocked the company sideways in an effort to meet the demand.

Ashton was also involved with the admag launch of Blue Band margarine, before the product's TV commercials. His idea for the script – on which everyone was sworn to utter secrecy – was the line, 'If you can spread this straight from the fridge, then I'm a monkey's uncle.' The margarine would be spread straight from the fridge; cue for the line from his screen partner, 'Have a peanut.' This sent the Kraft representative into a minor panic and he launched into a detailed explanation of why the word peanut, with its association with oil, could not be used as it would convey the wrong image.

Bernard Bresslaw, Clive Dunn and Mario Fabrizi appeared in a comedy admag for Harrison Gibson's department stores. The success of the series was demonstrated by the spectacular increase of shoppers on the day following

the programme. But when one customer complained to the managing director about a store of that calibre being associated with such low comedy, the admags were summarily cancelled. 6 foot 7 inches tall Bresslaw was compensated with a seven-foot bed.

John Slater, Noele Gordon, Spike Milligan and admag producer Alan Tarrant during a rehearsal break.

However, by mid 1961 the days of the small advertiser were numbered. The Pilkington Committee – set up in 1960 to report on British broadcasting – was rumoured to be viewing admags unfavourably. The rumours were more than borne out when the report appeared in June 1962. The Committee held that admags blurred the distinction between programmes and advertisements. 'In effect,' it stated, 'characters known to viewers as friendly personalities because they appear in regular programmes endorse, as though they were disinterested parties, the claims of the advertisers. They give the impression of having, on the most sensible homely grounds, decided to recommend this article rather than that.' (This despite the fact that all admags were announced as advertising material.)

The Committee's second complaint was that these programmes were, in fact, sponsored television, and that although they were made by the programme companies 'the impression made on the viewers' was of sponsorship.

Lastly, the Committee felt that admags increased the amount of television advertising time by far more than was envisaged in the ITA Act. On all these grounds, therefore, the Committee ruled that advertising magazines should be prohibited.

Although the government had not made the Committee's recommendation law, eleven out of fifteen programme companies dropped their admags within a few months. Rediffusion, who were the producers of 'Jim's Inn', 'On View' and special magazines based around the Ideal Home Exhibition and the Motor Show, as well as a particularly successful holiday special (which could draw up to three-quarters of a million replies via coupons in the *TV Times*), decided to wait until Parliament had ruled. The company had carried out a research survey which showed that 70% of its audience was in favour of its admags. Rediffusion's legendary general manager, the formidable Captain Tom Brownrigg, lobbied MPs in an attempt to halt the tide, but by the end of the year the Postmaster-General announced the ban. In retrospect the banning of admags seems an unnecessarily drastic action. Although some large advertisers took advantage of them for economy, they were tremendously useful to the smaller businesses. Colston dishwashers made their advertising debut in one magazine, and found they did not have the supply to cope with demand. On a much smaller scale was the Quickunpick stitch ripper. Even the British army advertised in admags.

In the introduction to the Pilkington Report the Committee made it clear that it was within its power to recommend that the ITA completely restructure its television service, possibly doing without advertising revenue altogether. A scapegoat was needed, and with the grand sentiment of 'We're only doing it for your own good' that pervades the report from beginning to end, the admags were sent into oblivion – despite the massive public outcry when 'Jim's Inn' was forced to join them.

The last products to be advertised in the STV admag 'Buy Lines' – presented by Sylvia Peters – were a range of canned convenience foods by Crosse & Blackwell. Designed to appeal to the shopper with a weakness for romantic-sounding names they included 'Beef Milano', 'Veal Sorrento', 'Beef Roma', 'Chicken Capri' and 'London Grill'. But only London Grill survives today.

Admags also survive – on every commercial television channel in Europe. This uniquely British invention, as far as the Continent is concerned, was one of the best ideas to come out of British commercial television.

PART 9

'The Lady is a Chimp'

TV Tea Spots

One of the earliest animal heroes in television was Congo, a chimp who appeared with Desmond Morris when he was a presenter on BBC-TV's 'Zoo Time' in the fifties. This was a long time before Morris explored man's fascination for certain animals in *The Naked Ape.*

But while Morris's ape was just a glimmer. Brooke Bond's then advertising agents were detailed to present an advertising campaign for the company's PG Tips tea. The adman responsible (so the legend goes) became so blocked for inspiration that he took a stroll through London's Regent's Park zoo, where he happened on a chimps' tea party and, with Archimedean delight, realized he had found the answer to the PG Tips campaign.

The first chimp commercial was screened in 1956. Set in an elegant country house, it showed two beautifully dressed 'girls' and 'boys' seated at a Regency table drinking tea from a silver service in dainty china cups. The chimps behaved like chimps, their actions delicately clumsy, while the voiceover – by Peter Sellers, who was paid £100 for the job – pointed up the contrasting gracious surroundings in a witty, upper-crust commentary. It was a vignette that could be shown today and enjoyed just as much.

After this very simple film the ideas became more ambitious, and chimps were shown playing in a jazz band and riding Ben Hur-style in chariots. These and others were to a predetermined storyline, the finished effect having been achieved by editing that gave a jumpy, clockwork action which is extremely primitive by today's standards. By the end of the sixties, the chimps were appearing in situation sketches along with live actors.

At about the same time, Brooke Bond began advertising tea bags along with their packet tea. Tea bags had proved difficult to establish in Britain, although they had been in use in the USA since the early part of the century. To Britons, however, the teapot was the inviolable centre of the tea ritual, to the extent of having its own share of tea in the process – 'And one for the pot,' as the last spoonful went in.

The unshakable conviction that loose-leaf tea could be substituted was hard to alter, but Tetley, who had been steadfastly marketing their tea bags since 1956 in a lone bid to rock packet tea, had succeeded in opening up the

1956: the first PG Tips chimp commercial.

Another early, more elaborate chimp set-up.

market sufficiently to interest PG Tips and Quick Brew (Lyons) in a share of the potential.

Teabag technology was less advanced in those days, and most manufacturers entering the market encountered problems. A major difficulty was the heat-sealing of the bags – if the sealant had too low a melting-point, the tea bag simply collapsed on its first contact with boiling water. Such an accident to the odd consumer's cuppa served only to reinforce prejudice about this new invention. Added to this, there was still a deal of ignorance about how tea bags should be used. Some thought it was a new way of packaging the tea in convenient quantities and snipped the bags open to pour out the contents; others agonized over the question of 'one for the pot' and whether the ruling applied to tea bags.

From 1969 until 1971, Brooke Bond rested the chimp commercials in some TV areas and tried other approaches. None succeeded as well as the chimps. From their national return in 1971 one man, Berny Stringle, has directed all their commercials (as well as hundreds for other products). His flair transformed the previous chimp formula from amusing sketches into full-scale simian situation comedy.

The completed commercials give no hint of the painstaking attention to detail that has gone before. The chimps are cast for their parts as if they were human actors and are trained to a script that will be dubbed by voiceovers when the film is complete. But filming the chimps takes between ten and fifty times longer than it would with humans.

Some weeks before filming, the chimps are given their props and trained to handle them. Their costumes are designed, but as chimps grow quickly, measurements are not taken until a month before filming. The chimpanzee's shape is a challenge to the designer. Chimps are extremely short-necked, long-armed, short-legged, narrow-shouldered and broad-chested. They are also very tough on the clothes, which means that light but durable cotton or wool are the most suitable fabrics. The clothes are double-seamed to withstand the extra wear and tear. Their shoes may look substantial enough on screen, but since it is essential that the chimps feel the ground through them they are made of very soft kid, which also fits comfortably on the animals' very wide, splayed feet.

The film sets and props are all scaled-down versions of the real thing, and members of the crew often add little touches of their own – creating more visual jokes. By the time shooting starts, the chimps will know more or less what is expected of them. They are rewarded with jelly babies, marshmallows and sweet, extra milky tea when they get the part right. But awkward moments are unavoidable – one chimp, supposed to be reading a magazine in the 'Costa Bombe' commercial, ate five copies before he could be persuaded to just look at it. In the 'Mr Shifter' ad the piano-playing chimp refused to use a dummy keyboard on the film set, but performed quite happily when the real one he had trained on was brought in. Incidentally, the 'Mr Shifter' sketch has now entered the record books as the most frequently televised commercial.

The cast in the 'Maternity Ward' commercial called for 'baby chimps', so a number of twelve-month-old chimps were used – chimp actors are usually in the four- to five-year-old age group. The 'babies' created utter confusion by constantly climbing out of their cots and scampering round the 'hospital ward' set.

When a particularly difficult shot is in the can, there is always a spontaneous burst of applause on the part of the crew for the chimp artists – a rare occurrence on most film sets, since crewmen are not easily impressed. At

Opposite: The record-breaker. 'Mr Shifter' minds the bannisters.

Davidson Pearce Berry and Spottiswoode Limited

67 Brompton Road, London SW3 1EF. Registered Office
Telephone 01-589 4595 Telegrams Inkling London. Telex 917744
Registered Number 102272 England

Client _____ BROOKE BOND OXO LIMITED _____   Length ___ 30 seconds _____

Product ___ PG Tips Packet Tea (Scotland)   Ref No ___ PG 67(30)/S _____

Title _____ "REMOVAL MAN" _____   Job No ___ TV 5395 _____

Script Identification ___ TRANSMISSION _____   Transmission Date _____

                                                   Date __ 31.1.78 _____

Picture	Sound
Open on CU of sign 'A. Shifter and Son, Removals'. Camera pulls out to reveal chimp in bowler hat and chimp with ginger wig trying to move a piano down the stairs into the hallway of a suburban house.	1½ seconds mute: BOWLER-HATTED CHIMP: Gettin' the hang of it? Mind the bannisters, son.
Cut to close up ginger chimp struggling with piano.	GINGER CHIMP: Ooh, I can't hold it, Dad.
Cut to close up of bowler-hatted chimp trying to shake piano	BOWLER-HATTED CHIMP: Don't worry son, I've shifted more pianos than you've had hot dinners
Cut to close up of ginger chimp still struggling.	GINGER CHIMP: Ooh!
Cut to close up bowler-hatted chimp.	
Cut to close up of ginger chimp. He looks downstairs.	LADY CHIMP: Cooee ....
Cut to mid shot looking down on lady chimp with tea trolley coming through door into hallway	...... Mr. Shifter, light refreshments.
Cut to close up of ginger chimp He leaves piano and falls out of frame.	

this the chimps always return the compliment by clapping their hands and jumping up and down.

The completed film is then dubbed, and over the years the chimps have acquired the vocal talents of many top entertainers. As well as Peter Sellers, Stanley Baxter, Denise Bryer, Fred Emney, Bruce Forsyth, Irene Handl, Arthur Lowe, Bob Monkhouse and Kenneth Williams have all contributed at various times.

The question that has to be asked of all popular commercials is whether they succeed in selling the product, and to this PG Tips need only point to their brand leadership in both the packet tea and teabag market. It could well be that rather than buying because of the commercials, people see the continuation of Brooke Bond's advertising on television as a reward for buying their products. What is certainly true is that the audience responds to the chimps as if to other human beings, because the situations and jokes in the commercials are very much a part of human experience. Just how far they can be forgotten as animals was illustrated when Brooke Bond were sent a script by someone who wanted a chimp to open a fête – and give a talk.

Berny Stringle admits wryly to a 'love/hate' element in his work with the chimps, because technically they are the hardest things he has ever directed. But as a film maker the more important consideration to him is the challenge that each new commercial represents, and nothing else he has done has half-way approached that posed by the chimps.

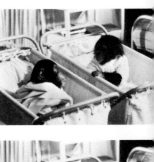
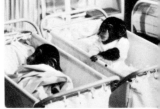
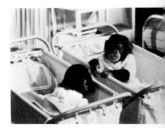
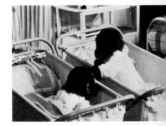

Peter Sellers during a recording of voices for the chimps at De Lane Lea B Recording Studio – now deserted – in Greek Street, London W1.

Above: Candid shots during the production of the 'Maternity Ward' commercial.

Opposite: Part of the shooting script for a PG Tips commercial.

Brooke Bond stopped using chimps in 1969 and went over to live-action sketches. But where the chimps had succeeded over the years in drawing laughs by gentle send-ups of many real-life situations, human actors were not accorded anything like the same tolerance. In January 1971, the company ran a series of commercials showing a vicar shopping in a supermarket. He was advised by a shop assistant to buy tea bags and replied, 'I don't think the Mothers' Union would like it'. The leaders of two branches of the Mothers' Union protested so vigorously at this slight on the organization that Brooke Bond were forced to withdraw the commercial.

Wisely, Brooke Bond brought the chimps back to the television screen later that year and have had no such trouble since. Absolute proof that while it is acceptable for chimps to make monkeys out of people, it is a bit risky for people to make monkeys of each other.

PART 10

'Glance at Our Old-Fashioned Ways'

Space Age Potatoes

Certain brand names have the power to evoke far more than the product they stand for because of associations with times, places and events. 'Pom' will still open the door to a host of wartime memories of the nameless Ministry of Food powdered potato substitute that formed part of the basic diet, along with dried eggs and dried fruit. It received the name 'Pom' after the war, but little else about it had changed.

In 1967 Cadbury/Typhoo presented their advertising agents with more than just a marketing problem when they asked them to plan a television campaign for Smash – a dried potato product that, with the addition of water, turned to instant mashed potato. It was a useful product – improved beyond recognition from that earlier staple – but the fresh potato habit would not be easy to break.

The first series of commercials showed couples or families eating mashed potato in various domestic situations, then being asked by the wife/girlfriend, 'How's the potato?' and answering that it was fine – as if it were no different than usual. The commercials had an infectious humour about them and ended with the voiceover asking, 'Have you tried it yet? Are you sure?'

The humorous touches broke the first barrier towards acceptability, and the next major television campaign took the bold step of showing the real potato as Smash's only serious rival. The visuals were basic – potato and packshot, with the case for using Smash put by the voiceover. Each film ended with a brilliant visual joke highlighting the disadvantages of real potatoes over the lighter, more convenient, dried kind. Along with these commercials was run, for the first time, the four-word jingle (music by Cliff Adams), 'For mash get Smash'.

Smash also had a go on a few occasions at its rivals in the instant potato market by mentioning that it had 'imitators'. These came within a whisker of the IBA's ruling on 'knocking copy'. (Paragraph 21: 'Advertisements should not unfairly attack or discredit other products, advertisers or advertisements directly or by implication.') The campaign was short-lived.

Smash then went into the space age, first of all showing astronauts eating

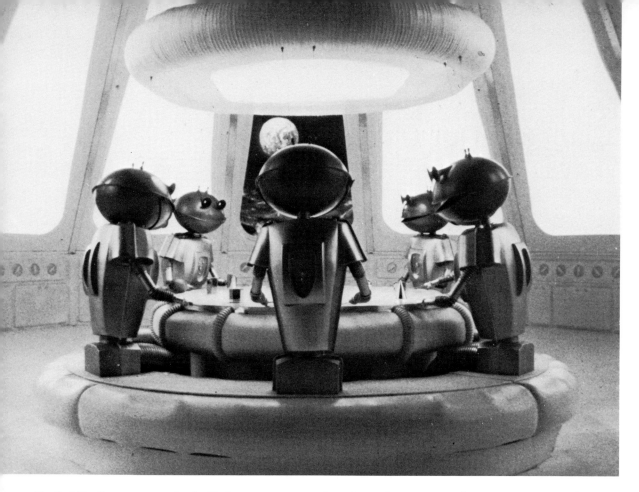

The first Martian summit: target – old-fashioned spuds.

food pills but insisting on Smash as their potato, then to a space-age kitchen where a mystified young woman (holding a potato) asks her mother, 'Have you seen one of these before?'

By this time Smash had beaten all its rivals for market leadership, and needed a long-running theme that would keep the product in the public mind and exclude all competitors. Humour was thought to be essential, as well as a regular group of characters of whom the viewers would become fond. Smash finally settled for neither animation nor animals but on robotic puppets who lived on Mars and were observers of the quaint habits of the people who inhabited Earth. They were particularly amused by the earth people's old-fashioned way of preparing and cooking potatoes.

The space age theme was just right for the middle seventies, but the appearance of the Martians was especially significant. Their heads were rounded, as were their eyes, and their mouths were large and upturned. Their first appearance showed them seated round a table discussing what the Earth people ate. In structure and movement – slightly lacking in fluidity – the Smash Martians were not so much metallic representations of space people as elemental chimpanzees. Heavy metal chimps.

Whatever influences worked on their creator either consciously or subconsciously, he had hit on a group of characters who could not fail to appeal because of the previous track record of the round-eyed, round-faced, wide upturned mouth archetype. Details of limbs and dress apart, the power of these main features is that they show the human face as it first appears to very young babies. This interpretation of the face lasts well into childhood, as children's drawings of people prove. It is a very unusual young child who does not start its drawing of a person with, first of all, a round face, eyes, nose and wide upturned line for the mouth.

Silver pinny, *de rigeur* for Martian mums.

Another aspect of the Martian theme of which its creator was quite unaware (because he had never seen the precursor) – the idea of people in space observing us on Earth – had been used over fourteen years previously by Nicholas Parsons in his commercials for Blue Car travel.

The Smash Martians were a hit from the start, and as more of the family, particularly the cat and dog, were brought into the plots their instantaneous success became firmly established. Fan mail for the Martians poured in to such an extent that the advertising agency had to prepare literature for the growing number of fans.

Denise Bryer and
husband Nicholas
Parsons observing the
habits of the Earth
people. This commercial
for Blue Car Travel won
the TV Mail Grand Prix
in 1961. It was directed
by Gerry Anderson, who
brought puppets into the
Space Age with
'Thunderbirds' and later
did the same with people
in 'Space 1990'.

Smash Martian meets
Earth person.

The *Smash Martians' Manual* was sent out in answer to the numerous requests for permission to use the characters in all kinds of merchandise. Potential exploiters of the Smash Martians have to follow the strict rules in the manual that detail every facet of the characters. In the section on the voice it states, 'The Smash Martians have very distinctive voices – clear diction with a metallic clip. Their laugh is infectious. They have only pleasant thoughts and would never utter an offensive statement,' and their size is a surprising 3 ft 6 ins – about the average height of a chimpanzee.

Technologically super-advanced the Martians may be, but they have a few old-fashioned ways. According to the *Smash Martians' Manual*, 'Mrs Smash is distinguished from Mr Smash by means of body props, e.g. pinny, hat, handbag, all in silver . . .'

Surely not pinnys all the time? What about their evenings out at the planetary local? But then Mars bars are probably different too.

PART 11

'Mr Wonderful'

Brand-Name Heroes

In twenty-five years of television commercials there has never been an anonymous woman whose very presence on the screen is immediately identified with a product. With men, however, it has been quite different. Since most of the twenty-five years have been spent aiming at the female purchaser, it was probably to be expected that a male macho symbol would be an attractive proposition.

The Lonely Man

The very first in this line, and often described as the greatest folk hero that ever came out of advertising, was Terence Brook, who in 1959 was sent by his agent to an ad agency seeking a very special kind of man to appear in a series of commercials. The advertiser was W. H. & D. O. Wills. The product was a new cigarette called Strand with a new-look flip-top pack.

Brook was interviewed – as were many others – by a board who were looking for a kind of detective/private eye character who would appeal to a younger audience. Shortly after his interview he was taken to dockland and photographed at night in overcoat and trilby hat. Having seen the result of this photo session the agency changed the concept of the character and decided he should convey the mood and look of Frank Sinatra in the film *Pal Joey*. The first commercial was shot outside Australia House at night. Brook wore a white overcoat, newly bought from Cecil Gee, together with a pull-down trilby.

Sensing that Terence Brook might attract some kind of popular following, the advertising agents decided just before the television launch to preview the commercial at a large London dance-hall. (It was quite common practice in the tobacco industry in the fifties and early sixties to promote cigarettes in dance-halls.)

For Brook, a jobbing actor until then, the event was part of another world. The dancing was stopped for an interval, then the MC stepped forward and announced to the dancers that Wills were launching a new cigarette on to the market and that they were to be shown the commercial that would be

Unforgettable Terence Brook . . .

it could have been Frank Sinatra.

Big Fry, big welcome.

appearing on their television screens soon. The commercial was shown and after it Terence Brook was led on stage, to the cry of 'Here he is in person.' Brook remembers having to distribute samples of Strand cigarettes to the audience before he left and the dancing recommenced.

When it appeared on the television screens in March 1960 the image of this slightly hunched figure, handsome in a haunting, undernourished way and wearing what appeared to be a battered trenchcoat and hat tilted – perhaps for disguise? – smouldered on to the television screen. Accompanying the visual was a notable piece of music (composed by Cliff Adams), and as the lone figure lit a cigarette the voiceover said, 'You're never alone with a Strand.' As an exercise in film and characterization the commercial was quite momentous.

More commercials were made – all on location – on the Thames embankment, in Bloomsbury, on Brighton seafront; one was memorable because the film company hired a Baker Street coffee bar (the Boccaccio)

Above and left: The Sandeman Don – otherwise actor Edwin Richfield.

Filmed two feet from the edge of Beachy Head, the guy who put the lager before the girl.

from midnight till 6 am to get the right setting.

While Terence Brook was coping with the increasing personal publicity which his 'lonely man' image had engendered, the press clamoured for news about him and his celebrity was such that many comedians used 'Strand situations' in their acts. The accompanying music, 'The Lonely Man Theme', received a lot of play on BBC radio (at a time, long before Radio One, when the BBC had perhaps only two disc jockeys of note.) The record was number 39 in the charts by the end of April 1960, and set to climb to the top, when the *News Chronicle* splashed a report that the BBC were helping to promote Strand cigarettes by playing the theme. Unlike today, when so many thinly diguised versions of the originals from commercials are played, the BBC in 1960 recoiled immediately from the taint of advertising and withdrew 'The Lonely Man Theme' (a straight orchestral piece) from its playlist. Without BBC radio playings, Cliff Adams and his UK Orchestra who had recorded the 'Theme' were denied a higher place in the charts, but they do have the distinction of producing the first-ever chart entry taken from a television commercial.

The Strand campaign ran for about eighteen months, and towards the end of that time word got out that the brand was selling badly and might even be dropped from Wills' range.

No other failed campaign in the history of television advertising has attracted the degree of post-analysis that followed Strand's fall from grace. The final verdict was the profoundly psychological interpretation that the audience did not want to identify with the solitary Strand-smoking hero because they too might be affected by his loneliness. It was as if 'You're never alone with [i.e. as long as you have] a Strand' meant the opposite.

But other factors indicated that the commercial was extremely popular. The Strand films had more in common with good cinema than the television screen and the TV audience had been reared on cinema. The theme music was popular and a potential hit. Terence Brook was popular, and his lean, boyish good looks were right out of the Sinatra mould.

With the acute sensitivity typical of the advertising world the agency blamed itself and no one since has attempted a campaign along the same lines. But by taking the blame there was an implied slight on the intelligence of the television audience – a hint that they were incapable of getting the message.

The product could have failed for a far more practical reason which no amount of talented advertising would have helped. Probably nothing can persuade people to continue to buy a product they do not want – except perhaps once.

The now-bearded Terence Brook is still acting, and has found a specialist

Opposite: As the Martini chauffeur, Ted Hemming drove some of Europe's top model girls around in this early-Sixties Martini ad.

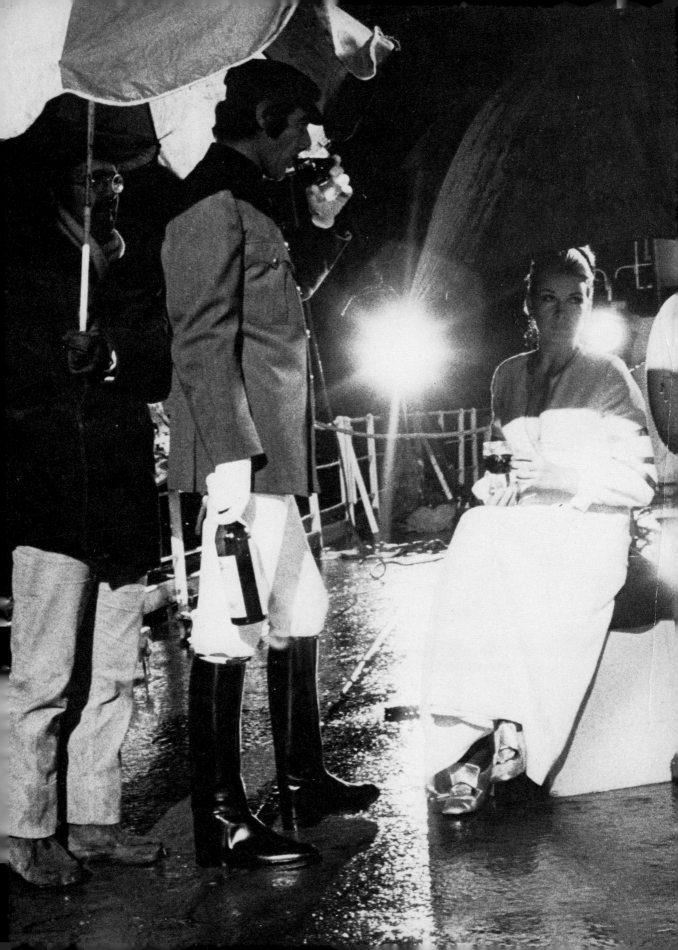

Randall Lawrence was the highly eclectic St Bruno man who spent much of his time in commercials cold-shouldering smouldering females. The hat was an unplanned prop. Sitting around in a tent in Tangier on the first day of the shoot (it was pouring outside) someone threw the cap over to him and he tried it on. It looked good and became his trademark – along with the pipe.

niche in the translation to English and production of nineteenth-century French plays by writers such as Alfred de Musset.

In the best heroic tradition, Brook went on to greater things.

Mark Vardy

The most intriguing hero in television commercials reversed all the standards by which a hero can be judged. As an actor he was never identified, his face was never seen, he received no publicity; but his presence had a greater reality for each individual who saw him. His first appearance was in a campaign just before Christmas 1961. His name, 'Mark Vardy' – which was also the name of the product.

The evolution of 'Mark Vardy' began when Beecham's contemplated expanding their men's toiletry range to include more than just after-shave. The venture needed very careful planning, as there would obviously be very high resistance from men. A row of bottles in the bathroom was nothing exceptional for women in 1961 but the self-image of men was much more spartan.

Naming the product was the first major hurdle. The name had to express masculinity and have a slightly American ring. After a myriad of suggestions Beecham's found that one of their directors – Mark Vardy – possessed the ideal name. He gave permission for it to be used and the commercial went into preparation.

The search for a man to play 'Mark Vardy' began. He had to be tall with a good strong head and profile and, very importantly, he had to be able to walk with the suggestion of a limp. This last condition was an essential part of the character-file which had been drawn up for Vardy, and was intended to convey the impression that he had at one time sustained an injury in some suitably masculine sport – motor racing, possibly. Young actor Steve Hudson had all the qualities required and landed the part.

The original concept called for Mark Vardy to walk (back to camera) between two rows of symbols of the jet age (i.e. a jet engine, turbine, etc.). The rows were to diminish in perspective, and at the end a woman would appear from the right and they would walk away while he turned the merest profile towards her. The film was to be shot at Cinéaste studios in Paris (where Brigitte Bardot made most of her early films and was then working on her latest). Because of the Paris location the jet-age idea had to be abandoned as impracticable and the 'symbols' were to be replaced with female statues – which proved equally unworkable. It was finally decided to use real women to portray the statues (this was long before the days when 'special effects' companies came into being to produce whatever was needed to solve this kind of problem). It took some considerable effort to pose the women in a way that would not upset the ITA, and the final effect was achieved using white powder from head to foot, white wigs and leotards.

The finished film was stunning as 'Mark Vardy' walked (back to camera) between the statues and at the end walked off with the woman who appeared from behind a pillar, turning that slight profile as he did so. The background music track was a compelling drumbeat while the voiceover (supplied by the producer, Chris Eaton) intoned, 'Mark Vardy – Mark Vardy – Mark Vardy is for men.' There then followed a list of the products in the MV range – soap, talc, after-shave and deodorant.

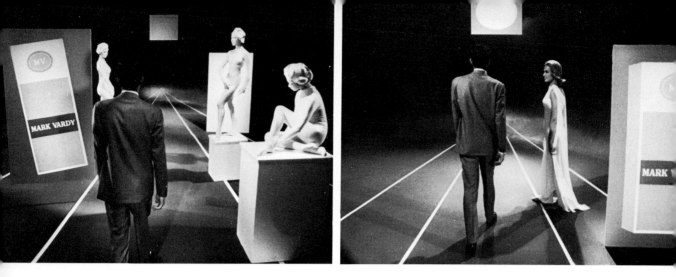

'Mark Vardy' begins his walk. This shot is heavy with symbolism – the lines meeting in the distance can also be seen as a pyramid. The square in the distance (the MV label is indistinct in this still) is compellingly placed. It could be a window to outside or an obstacle to be overcome. As he passes the last female 'statue' a real woman appears – the viewer can see her react to his appearance.

The campaign was a runaway success and Christmas stocks of 'Mark Vardy' disappeared from the shelves as fast as they were replaced. Women were the main purchasers – probably quite unaware of the effect that anonymous man had had on them. The use of a hero without a face was made with deliberate psychological intent. The television 'Mark Vardy' was a canvas left just blank enough for the individual viewer to imprint on it, at a subconscious level, an image of the ideal man.

There are conflicting accounts of why the product was dropped in 1962. Perhaps the product was ahead of its time. And the commercial – even in 1980 – is still.

As for the man who played the hero, he went on to specialize in voiceover work. 'Mark Vardy' is now the voice behind commercials for Old Spice . . .

Big Fry

The next male hero emerged in the middle sixties, a tall, dark, handsome and extrovert character called Big Fry (played by Australian actor George Lazenby). His role in commercials for Fry was that of a beefcake Santa Claus, with the muscle power to carry wooden crates crammed with chocolate bars to wherever the lucky recipients waited – on clifftops, mountain sides, harbours – to greet him with a delighted 'Big Fry!', after which began the chorus:

> Big Fry is back in town
> Big Fry
> Big Fry is back in town
> Big Fry
> Bigger bars – same price
> Bigger bars – same price
> Big Fry is back in town

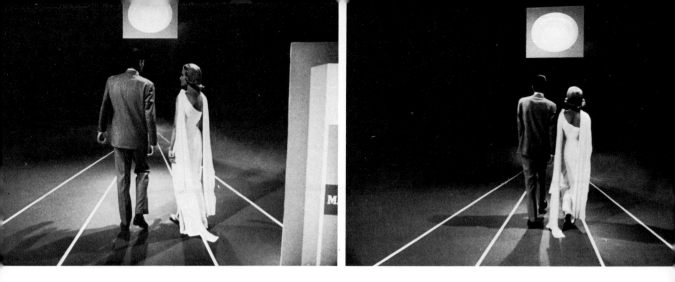

Big Fry's prices were pretty good in his pre-decimal day – Turkish Delight cost 6d for the small bar and 9d for the bigger bar.

Big Fry was a handy device for reminding people of Fry's chocolate bar range, as he would shift different bars in each commercial and sometimes the whole range at once.

The big difference between Big Fry and other commercial heroes was his complete lack of mystery. The role hinged on his being recognized wherever he went, but this familiarity began to detract from his heroic appeal. The absence of mystery worked against Big Fry's credibility, and the character became almost something of a joke.

Big Fry did have the edge on the rest of the commercial heroes because he went on to become – no matter how brief the span – *the* hero of the cinema screen, James Bond, after Sean Connery had given up the role. Interestingly, George Lazenby's departure after only one Bond film left the way open for two other commercial heroes to test for the part. Both Steve Hudson (Mark Vardy) and Gary Myers (of whom more later) made it to the final short-list – only to be beaten to it by Roger Moore.

But the vacancy left by Lazenby for a new Big Fry did not need to be filled. The campaign was dropped.

Left: This key frame shows just how little of Vardy's face was revealed, but the woman is obviously very happy with what she can see. The female audience now identifies with what she sees in the man.

Right: The tantalizing walk away. Where? To what? The structure of the film is meshed with possibilities. An intricate psychological jigsaw.

The Cloak Factor

Although they do not strictly belong to the hero category, there were two major television campaigns featuring cloaked figures. Sandeman's port brought their trademark, the Spanish Don, to the screen in a long series of 'Find the Don' commercials. And in the early seventies, with the copy line of 'Thirst things first', Harp lager ran a television campaign showing a cloaked figure who drank the lager before he kissed the girl. This man of mystery was played by a slightly more visible Steve Hudson – last unseen as Mark Vardy.

'And all . . .   because . . .

The Man of Mystery

It is hard to believe that the last in the list of commercial heroes has been appearing since 1968 and in terms of heroism he is the undoubted leader.

Back in 1968, Cadbury's were completely revamping their television advertising for Milk Tray chocolates. Their previous commercials had usually stressed the romantic associations of chocolates with present-giving; pleasant, soft-centred stuff. Now embarking on a new campaign, their advertising agents informed all likely sources – including model agencies – that they were looking for a man with a 'special image'. They knew what they were looking for, they said, but could not put it down exactly. The man had to be tall and dark and the possessor of a certain indefinable magic.

At that time there were around ten model agencies in London (the figure is now about thirty) and all searched their files for likely candidates, putting in as many as they could for audition. No one knew what he was auditioning for, but that kind of uncertainty is one of modelling's occupational hazards.

Gary Myers, a protégé of Tom Sheridan who runs the International Model Agency Ltd, was chosen for the part which, it was revealed, called for a James Bond-type who would be involved in high adventure. And that was no understatement. The campaign was to be on the line, 'And all because the lady loves Milk Tray,' and each new commercial involved the hero in even

the lady loves . . .   Milk Tray'

greater feats of daring so that he could reach the lady's home with the box of chocolates and that calling card.

When he started in 1968, Gary Myers did quite a bit of the stuntwork himself – as an expert swimmer, surfer and all-round sportsman he was eminently capable. But as the years went on and his value as the hero increased, the most dangerous stunts were given to stuntmen.

In addition to Gary Myers and the stunts, the atmosphere of excitement and danger in each film was heightened by the accompanying music, the first bars of which immediately evoked a sense of mystery and adventure. Cliff Adams was again responsible for the composition and orchestration.

Most surprisingly, Myers has retained the complete anonymity he had from the very first commercial for the twelve years the campaign has lasted. As long as the lady continues to love Milk Tray, Gary Myers will deliver without any fear of becoming a familiar face. For twelve years the viewing audiences have only ever seen him in profile.

No cinema hero in recent times has ever matched James Bond, still comparatively earthbound while space movies laser away at his popularity. When the last Bond film *is* made, there may be just one screen hero left to epitomize courage and quick thinking in the face of natural danger.

And he will be carrying a box of chocolates in his hand.

PART 12

'K-K-K-Katie'

The Big Story of a Little Cube

When Oxo began advertising on television the product was already forty-five years old. In the middle of the nineteenth century Baron von Liebig, a German philanthropist, discovered a method of extracting the concentrated goodness of cattle meat and, having perfected this process, offered it to whichever company would use it to the benefit of society.

A group of businessmen willing to set up a company approached him and,

Oxo's first TV appearance

as 'Liebig's Extract of Meat Co.', sold the product in jars from 1865. In 1910 the company took the processing even further, making the extract into cubes, and these went on sale for a penny. Packed in individual cartons the cubes were named Oxo, the shipping mark on the sacks of meat compound from Argentina. Between 1914 and 1918 the cubes were sold in sixes and grosses, as they were part of rations for most British soldiers. In the Second World War too, Oxo was a vital food for the troops.

Up until the mid 1950s Oxo's advertising was earnest and austere, and the very first Oxo commercial, 'Millions of Cubes', echoed Oxo's wartime role by showing an endless stream of animated Oxo cubes marching through the countryside behind the leader, who held an Oxo banner.

The next campaign took the product into the 'fun' category by presenting it through television's most popular puppet of the fifties, Sooty, along with his handler Harry Corbett.

Then came Katie, whose job was to promote Oxo and cooking together. In the early days she could be seen three times in one evening. At seven o'clock she would appear, introduce herself and explain what she was going to cook. By 8.30 there would be another Katie break at which she would announce that the meal was nearly ready, and at the end of the evening she would appear for the last time, mainly to plug the Oxo meat cookery book.

Katie, with Philip and latterly their son David – who arrived quite suddenly, neither Katie or Philip having mentioned the happy event and with no hint from Katie's figure that she was carrying more than her usual helping of meat with Oxo gravy – were eagerly followed by their audience

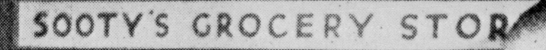

and attracted high praise from television critic Peter Black. Writing in the *Daily Mail* in January 1962 he noted, 'Some commercials are so well made that although they last only a minute and involve their personages in a single incident, they seem to create a world as detailed as that of any of the soap operas.' Black went on to speculate about their background, parents, schools, etc., and wondered whether the Philip and Katie series would ever make the top ten most popular commercials. 'I'm pretty sure they wouldn't,' he concluded. 'There is too much about them that is like real life. For the curious thing about commercials, which as far as I know I alone have noticed, is that the audience applies to them the reverse of the values it applies to the programmes.' If Black's observation was correct, then it must follow that Katie and Philip were seen more as a programme than as a commercial.

The characters were as carefully drawn as if they had been in a programme series, with just the lack of delineation that had set Peter Black speculating. Katie was a housewife and mother and good at entertaining –

A shot from the Oxo commercial which won first prize at the International Advertising Film Festival in Monte Carlo, 1956.

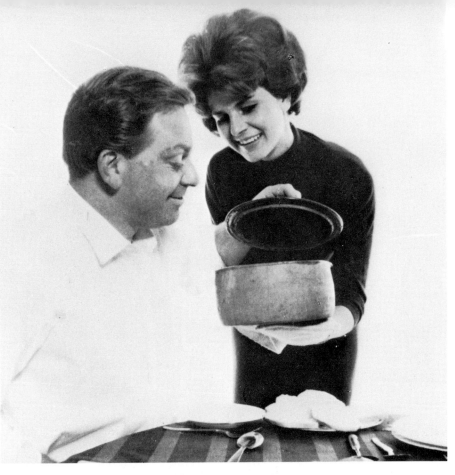

Katie and Philip, an early Oxo meal. Katie was played by Mary Holland (she eventually changed her name to Katie Holland); Philip was actor Peter Moynihan.

Katie and son at the local shop. Son David was played by Keith Berriman.

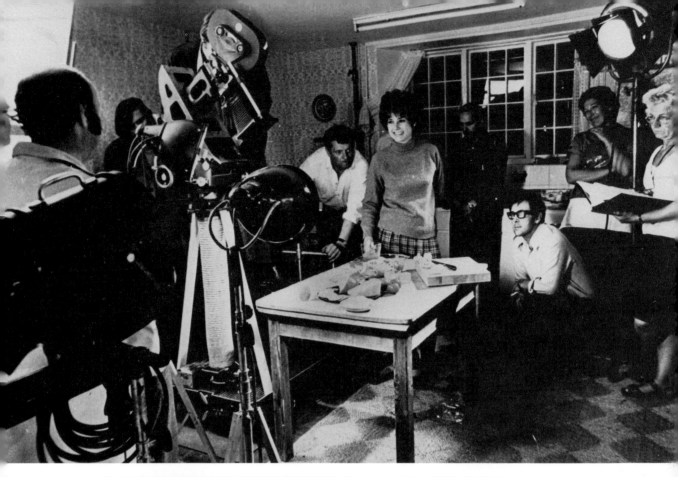

The country house set

Thoroughly modern
Katie

she first served wine with meals in 1958. Philip had some kind of job that meant being present at building sites. He could have been anything from an architect, surveyor, to site foreman – the viewer could decide.

The couple progressed from that early town kitchen to a country house in Northumberland when society at large was beginning to feel the call back to nature. The family then went to the USA. This trip was of course a marketing decision, putting Katie in a situation where she would be explaining Oxo to people unfamiliar with the product (i.e. her new American friends) while restating the Oxo message to the TV audience.

In 1972 when there was a downturn in the British economy Katie and Co. were recalled from the States, and the emphasis in the subsequent commercials was how to cook better with less. Cheaper cuts of meat were used and Katie showed she could still keep 'a hungry man happy' with liver and leeks – and Oxo gravy.

In 1974 the axe finally fell on the Oxo family after eighteen years. Katie, still as warm and attractive as ever, had to go. There were protests at the news, but no begging letters to the company as experienced by Birdseye when their Ben went off to Australia. Oxo wanted a fresher image – but cannily kept Katie on in the Harlech area for comparison. Katie's residency at Harlech finished at the end of 1976, but she stayed with Oxo for a year after that on promotional work.

The crumble

Dennis Waterman and Oxo T-shirt – a very appealing combination.

When Oxo reappeared it was with the crumble sign, which soon achieved folk gesture status. The commercials showed lorry drivers, scaffolders and children twiddling two fingers and a thumb, and before long Oxo lorry drivers found they were being given the crumble sign by passing motorists. Oxo representatives at exhibitions would be greeted in the same way.

Late in 1977 Dennis Waterman appeared as the son whose mum was worried he wasn't eating well enough. The Oxo T-shirt he wore resulted in sackloads of requests to the company requesting the same. A similar response was fired by the Oxo mugs, and for a while the company doubted whether they were selling mugs, T-shirts or Oxo cubes.

Oxo's message to take the cube into the eighties is the bright and racy 'Only Oxo does what only Oxo can' – which almost suggests that at some point in the future this 'rose is a rose' statement may well need explaining to the generation who never had a Katie to show it what Oxo *can* do.

PART 13

'You Took Advantage of Me'
Women in TV Commercials

Katie disappeared from commercials just too soon to merit consideration as a 'woman' in a 'commercial' in the way that is now compelling advertisers to take note of how women are portrayed. The growth of feminism in the seventies and the increasing consciousness of women about their own identity – which eventually extended beyond the individual so that a slight on one woman was taken as a slight on womankind and had to be fought as such – led to the formation of 'Women in the Media'. Because the group consisted of women working in channels of communication – press, magazines, radio and television – their intention was to act as vigilantes in the battle against the 'exploitation' and 'humiliation' of women.

In May 1979, at a much publicized event held at the restaurant in London's Regent's Park zoo Women in the Media presented their 'Ad Lib' award for the least sexist commercial to the ad for Skyline kitchenware, which showed 'an unglamorous middle-aged couple working happily together in the kitchen'. Their 'Ad Nauseam' award was presented to Fiesta kitchen towels for a commercial which portrayed 'the ad man's cheaply-shaped stereotype of the housewife'. The Fiesta commercial – where a wife smeared a sticky mess over her husband's head as a prelude to showing how well Fiesta towels can mop up – could well be said to have degraded women. It was also a deeply humiliating experience for the husband, and possibly represented some misbegotten attempt on the part of the advertiser to respond to the accusation that women were always made to look silly, by turning the tables.

In May 1976 the Rape Crisis Centre claimed that television advertising could give men the idea that girls secretly yearn for the caveman approach, perhaps resulting in more cases for the centre to cope with. They were especially concerned over a commercial for Supersoft hairspray that showed a group of 'Vikings' looting a 'Saxon' village, ending with one of the village girls being carried away protesting by a 'Viking' raider.

But for organized protest on the image of women in commercials, nothing has approached a survey of unparalleled thoroughness conducted back in 1963 by the Townswomen's Guilds in South Wales. The monitoring of

television and commercials by all 1,000 members began in October 1962. Thereafter, for six solid months the members watched and noted. Their comments after this marathon view-in were submitted to the three area leaders, who prepared reports for a conference on the subject which was held in April 1963.

A Mrs D. M. Stratton of Neath summed up the complaints of so many: 'We are convinced', she said, 'that the advertisers and producers believe we viewers are nothing but morons.'

Mrs V. Stanley of Cardiff elaborated. 'We accept that all advertising is exaggeration, but some of it is so stupid that it irritates us and breeds consumer resistance to the products shown, as does the constant repetition of advertising.' 'Women could tell Stork from butter,' she added, 'and they were not taken in by Brand X which washed the whitest of them all, nor by the sight of the Duke of Bedford's Flash-clean floor.'

These middle-aged identical twins featured in commercials for McDougall's flour shown in the Yorkshire area in 1959. They shine out as extraordinarily ordinary.

Mrs Stanley continued, less damningly, to say that some advertisements, particularly the humorous ones, were quite enjoyed and admitted that members tapped their feet 'to some of the gay jingles'.

The third area leader, Mrs G. Starr from the Gwent and Wye area, complained of 'an over-emphasis on violence' and of 'everlasting sex' in too many plays and films. She wished, she said, that romance was made pleasant for a change. Interestingly the women of South Wales made no mention of the bodily exploitation of women or their use as 'sex objects' – a cause of protest in later years – but rather concentrated on the abuse of female intellectual ability.

Whatever faults the first ten years of television commercials may have had, they were not only more truly reflective of women but also of womanpower. Independent Television started just ten years after the end of a war which placed great value on the female contribution.

In many of Birdseye's early commercials a housewife is interviewed by a reporter about her purchases. The reporter is a woman. Again in Birdseye's fifties' campaigns, a young housewife explains that she has to go out to work and finds Birdseye products convenient for an easy meal in the evening.

In 1962, Beecham's ran a Horlicks commercial that showed two women taking part in a motor car rally – one driving, one navigating. They win the race and the last shot is of the driver holding aloft the trophy. Seventeen years before 'Women in the Media' it sounds like an unattainable ideal, but Beechams were reflecting part of a time when drivers like Pat Moss and Sheila van Damm were international rally champions.

If a commercial called for a studio presenter it was just as likely to be a woman as a man – they were regarded as equally authoritative.

One Hotpoint commercial from the end of the fifties – and in twenty-five years of Independent Television one of the most amazing sixty seconds' worth there has been – used a new angle for its 'no tangle action', USP (Unique Selling Point), and had a presentation from a laboratory that handled radioactive material. The woman presenter, wearing an obligatory white coat, introduced viewers to another of Hotpoint's tests to prove that 'Hotpoint washes cleaner because it cannot tangle clothes.' The male voiceover then introduced the location, 'Isotope Developments Ltd' (an invented name for a real lab), and described what was happening on screen. A solution was prepared mixing a radioactive isotope with a strongly adhesive grease. This concoction was then smeared in equal quantities over two identical pieces of cloth. The cloths were tested with geiger counters for radioactivity, then one was placed in a Hotpoint machine and the other in a machine without a 'no tangle action'. After a thorough wash, both cloths were re-tested for radioactivity – the Hotpoint-washed cloth now registered

Left: 'More pie in the tin and Mum knows best!' was the copyline for this 1960 commercial for Walls steak and kidney pie. The 'mum' image has altered radically in twenty years.

Right: An early commercial for *Woman* magazine in the London area proved so popular that viewers would ring the television company on Wednesday evenings to ask when the commercial would be shown. This was at a time when TV commercials had regular weekly spots. The presenter was the 'cover girl'.

Left: Another woman presenter in 1959 explained the advantages of renting a TV set from DER.

scarcely a crackle on the geiger counter while the other remained highly radioactive. All the laboratory staff on screen were women and they were conducting the experiment for real. The woman then in charge of the campaign remembers having to be checked for radioactivity on her visits to supervise filming. Playing around with isotopes may have been a piece of overselling, but it did show women as competent, efficient, scientific workers.

The first ten years were notable, too, for the absence of the cliché casting that has become a stereotype. Most chocolate products and sweets seem to be consumed today by women and children – apart from that chunky Yorkie bar which is more firmly installed than the tachograph in the cabs of Britain's truckers. But the Crunchie slogan used to be 'Be a Crunchie man', worlds removed from Crunchie's more recent 'golden moments' as experienced by wistful lady crunchers. Toffee Crisp was the 'big-sized munch from Mackintoshes', and Picnic was a 'man-sized munch'. When Cadbury's launched Bar 6 to rival Kit-Kat with the slogan, 'The only way to enjoy Bar 6 is to eat it yourself' the unsharing nibbler was a man.

The longest-running of all TV commercials, Fry's Turkish Delight, did undergo a radical change from 1969, reversing the trend and portraying women more positively. Fry's could well plead authenticity for the slave-woman view its commercials showed in the campaign's early years. The first Turkish Delight ad had a male slave carrying in a large carpet which he unrolled before the throne of a handsome Eastern potentate, thereby revealing the beautiful young captive, hidden Cleopatra-like inside. The woman, immediately submissive, ran to the prince's feet and began feeding him pieces of Turkish Delight.

As the Fry's campaign progressed and the films shifted to outdoor locations the woman was allowed more action – running up dizzily steep castle steps, braving horse charges, tribal skirmishes, fire and potential attackers, with the sweetmeat bowl firmly in her hands to deliver the precious oriental confectionery to her master. These commercials predated and prestyled the 'All because the lady loves Milk Tray' advertising for Cadbury, making a woman the hero figure until the inevitable final frames when she had to wield the sweet fork.

With their change to colour in 1972 the Turkish Delight commercials completely reversed the male/female roles, presenting the woman as the principal figure watching the men engage in various feats of combat and ending with the victor running to the woman's feet.

Fry's Turkish Delight commercials were designed from the outset to appeal to escapist fantasies, and it is a curious fact that sales of the product were traditionally greater in South Wales than any other part of the British Isles.

The Cadbury's Milk Flake commercials of the sixties were far removed from the dreamy focus of the seventies and eighties. Their presentation had an impressive realism. Shot in black and white by Keith Ewart – a key exponent of the use and knowledge of film, whose contribution to commercial film making played a major part in advancing techniques – the Milk Flake girls appeared in a variety of natural locations: a riverside, a rose garden, an Irish donkey cart, a country lane in the rain. The films communicated unqualified naturalism and a delight in the product. The young women emerged as credible people dressed in ordinary clothes in identifiable surroundings.

From chocolate bars to soap, and in the early sixties there was the equality of BO.

Cy Endfield – who went on to direct *Zulu* – shot some revolutionary footage for Lifebuoy, the soap that vanquished BO. Each commercial showed either two male or female friends out (in all kinds of locations) to have a good time and attract a likely partner. When one of the pair is seen to be a walking turn-off, the other whispers helpfully – in that classic parody of confidence – BO. This was all that was needed for the offender to rush to the bath and scourge his body with Lifebuoy.

Cy Endfield made his bath shots the more revealing by inserting a shot in which the opaque bath panel was suddenly made transparent – by substituting glass. This gave a virtual head to toe shot of the naked body, whether male or female. A clever device that treated the sexes equally, regardless of criticism that it was in doubtful taste.

Yeastvite tablets went as far as to acknowledge that 'Every working mother has three faces' (one for herself, one for her children and one for her husband).

Flash cleanser, in its 'All round the house spring clean with Flash' campaigns, showed both men and women doing just that, and the early Dulux commercials similarly represented an equal division of labour when painting the house.

Such sex symbols as existed in commercials from the mid fifties were mainly reserved to promote the sales of petrol. Both Fenella Fielding (too well loved to be a *sex* symbol), who oboed her praise of BP Superformance 'For the car in your life,' and Caroline Sanders, the Regent cowgirl, brought more than a hint of suggestion in their way with a petrol pump.

In 1966 there were commercials aimed to get more women to visit pubs. Novelist Monica Dickens was shown meeting a female friend at the local and expressing her enjoyment of the visit. In 1967 it was the turn of Mr and Mrs Hammond Innes (novelists seemed to be highly sought-after persuaders). Also that year women were seen to purchase stout in a commercial for Ansell's Goldcrest.

Two shots from a 1962 commercial for Horlicks. In one a woman drives while her partner navigates. The second shot shows the female winners.

1965 to 1967 were the transitional years, the time when 'pop music' was really acknowledged as more than a fleeting phenomenon, and changing fashions accompanied the new music. Advertisers had nodded in the direction of pop music in 1963 when cartoon Beatles were used to launch Nestle's Jellimallo bar. The Rolling Stones provided the musical backing for an animated graphics commercial for Rice Krispies, which was done in a 'Juke Box Jury' parody. A 1963 live-action commercial for Quaker Puffed Wheat mixed the talents of Craig Douglas, Cliff Richard, Acker Bilk and Lonnie Donegan with a voiceover by Brian Matthew (who was Mr Pop at the BBC), combining to promote Puffed Wheat as a 'swinging way to start the day'. Between 1963 and 1965 there appeared a rash of ads for publications – *Valentine, Princess, Fabulous, Jackie* and *TV Comic* (with pop stars) – targeted at a market which was scarcely comprehended.

A glimpse of the 'typical 1955 teenager' showing the winner
of the 'Girl of the Year' competition organized by *Heiress*
magazine. The winner was eighteen years old.

An early-Sixties
Cadbury's Milk Flake girl.

But the key commercial of 1965, the pivot around which every wish-fulfillment woman has circled ever since, was the launch of a hair colourant called Sea Witch. The Sea Witch women were not at all like women of this world. With challenging eyes, flowing hair and clothes like exquisite rags, they lit several million fantasies. An unnamed observer (from the world of advertising) wrote in *Television Mail*, 'Women love to be witches, so half the name of this new product is well thought up. Is it to be the first of a series selling through mythology?' Not only was it the first but its influence has remained ever since.

Significantly the Sea Witch style was reinforced with the help of music and fashion. As fashion changed and women revealed more of their bodies, particularly with the advent of the mini-skirt, photographers and film makers were quick to take advantage of the opportunity to produce more provocative images.

And with dancing becoming less of a social activity and more a medium for self-expression, women's inhibitions about their bodies tended to be gradually discarded. But each new freedom women gained carried with it the risk that others might exploit it. Like the 'Newton's Cradle' principle, every progressive action presented an equal and opposite reaction.

It is, however, to women's advantage that they are becoming more difficult to classify, as boundaries between age groups, occupation and class – those advertisers' stand-bys – blur into uncertainty.

Schweppes found this to their cost in 1969 when they launched on television a vodka-based drink called Tiara. The commercials were carefully designed to appeal to women in the C1/C2 (i.e. lower end of the economic scale) category. The product never took off.

A 1970 campaign for Shredded Wheat drew some embittered comments from women. Writing about the campaign in *The Observer* (29 March 1970),

1965: the first amazing Sea Witch commercial. Women in commercials would never be the same again.

Jeremy Bugler called it a 'good example of the place of women in advertising. It is the women who are important, not the men. This is mainly', he continued, 'because of the greater purchasing importance of the housewife. In short, advertising man has had a long and placid flirtation with advertised woman.' Bugler then reported how the women's liberation movement, 'a newish but growing campaign', found the portrayal of women in advertising 'sticks in the throat' and 'forces women into playing a role'.

Two surveys conducted sixteen years apart provide a glimpse of the change that has occurred within that span.

In 1961 the *Daily Express* asked 1,450 housewives what they did during commercial breaks:

30% were either knitting, sewing or darning
19% were doing household chores
8% were looking after children
13% were cooking
7% were eating
23% were watching the screen

In 1977 *The Financial Times* conducted a similar survey over 1,300 random households and found:

27% left the room (19% to go to the kitchen)
20% went to the bathroom
3% put the children to bed
50% were watching the screen

The increase in the number of women with the time to watch commercials is considerable – and it would be a foolish advertiser who risked the alienation of such a large audience.

Writing on 'Women and Advertising' in 1977, Roderick White, marketing director of Lansdowne Marketing Ltd, put it very simply.

Even allowing for the long-standing place of the insult, both verbal and physical, in British humour, it doesn't always appear to be a very promising procedure to insult the people you are hoping to sell to. All that can be said about this sort of approach is that if you feel insulted, the advertiser will lose a lot of money.

How very different the women's fight has been from the lone plea of TV critic Philip Purser.

Writing in 1965 about the similarities in the 'Katie and Philip' Oxo campaigns and the BBC situation comedy 'Marriage Lines', he had concluded,

Wasn't the husband's role in both instances awfully immature, even rather silly? Wasn't the favourite posture a rueful one, with hubby caught out by wifey and having to hang his head boyishly and a bit mischievously, so that she – and with her, every soft-hearted female in the audience – could only pretend to be cross? Wasn't the appeal to the maternal instinct, and isn't it about time we had a more assertive, grown-up image for the national husband?

PART 14

'Mean to Me'

Breaking the Colour Bar

One minority which has no pressure-group to support its claim to fair treatment in television commercials is Britain's black minority. In this case the claim would not be for misrepresentation but rather, until quite recently, nil-representation. Not only did black actors and actresses fail to appear in commercials throughout most of the years of Independent Television, they also had scant opportunity for appearing on television at all.

The ITA received regular letters in the early sixties from one correspondent who felt black people were getting a raw deal in commercials. In 1962 the same writer noticed a black girl in a commercial for Polo mints and wrote to say if it could happen once it could be possible again.

Certain commercials managed to highlight the situation, albeit unwittingly, by for example naming two housewives doing comparative tests, Mrs Black and Mrs White. Flash floor cleanser used this kind of advertising method repeatedly by showing 'Mrs Black' and 'Mrs White' washing a kitchen floor – one using Flash, (always Mrs White) and the other a useless substitute (always Mrs Black or, sometimes, Brown). At the end of the ad, Mrs White would emerge as sensible and efficient while the voiceover would sympathetically encourage Mrs Black to give Flash a try.

This type of advertising continued unchallenged for many years, like the endless rerun of some hack western movie with the villain in a black hat and the good guy in white. It took until the fringe of 1980 for Flash to name their comparative housewives without ambiguity.

What could have been a breakthrough in this discriminatory state of affairs occurred in 1965 when a preview critic saw a commercial for Spiller's Homepride flour. The ad featured a black cook and the critic wrote in *Television Mail*: 'This is the first time I remember seeing a coloured artist in a commercial. If others are as good as this one, let's see some more.'

However, not only did the critic not see more; in common with the rest of the television audience he never saw the Spiller's commercial again. It was inexplicably dropped.

Commercials managed to reach the seventies without the benefit of black participants until an American correspondent for *Variety* split the silence on

the subject and slammed this blinkered policy in public. Observing that black people were not seen in British television commercials the reporter said, 'You don't even see a tinted face lurking in the back of a crowd shot or picking up fares in a bus, despite the fact that over recent years that job (and other lower-rung chores) has been forfeited to immigrant blacks.'

For the Independent Television Authority, Archie Graham replied:

We have no attitude. One would hope that coloured people would turn up as a natural thing. I once went to America where they were casting a lot of black people in commercials regardless (*sic*). But I found this spread resentment among coloured people who, seeing themselves in AB [top of the economic scale] situations – split ranch houses etc., that sort of thing – thought they were being got at.

The *Guardian* newspaper, which had picked up the *Variety* correspondent's

A rare appearance by non-white actors in the first years of TV commercials. The shot is from an early Fry's Turkish Delight production session.

report, went on to point out the well-trodden 'fields in which they [black people] have been quietly and unostentatiously getting on'.

America's experience of black integration into television and commercials had been quite a recent development, initiated by the Kennedy regime in the early sixties. A statutory policy of tokenism was introduced which meant that television shows were bound to include black artists and members of the audience in numbers proportionate to the white representation on the shows. Although the policy was derided in certain quarters – many British commentators included – it did lead to full and natural integration on American television.

In December 1971 a British TV commercial for Coca-Cola featured a multi-racial choir (drawn from various embassies in Rome) singing 'I'd Like to Buy the World a Coke'. Because of the immense popularity of not only the commercial but the subsequently released single 'I'd Like to Teach the World to Sing', it went some way to establishing a place for other than white faces on the television screen. By now, BBC children's television had made good their earlier lack of black artists, notably in 'Playschool'.

Research on the number of black applicants to appear in public participation TV game shows has demonstrated the importance of audience identification with the people they see on television. Where a show has previously included a black contestant, others seem to be encouraged to

Being part of a send-up means you have really made it. This marvellous spoof on the Astaire classic *Top Hat*, first shown in Spring 1980 was nothing but good news.

Opposite: Action and teamwork from this late-Seventies Midland Bank commercial, and a significant step forward in black representation.

apply. But when the contestants are invariably white the black population practises a kind of self-exclusion by accepting the status quo – rarely, if ever, requesting the chance to appear.

But the three years from 1978 to date have seen a major turnabout in the employment of black people in television advertising, to the extent that television commercials have taken the lead in reflecting a multi-racial Britain. It must, to the advertisers, make good marketing sense, and for Britain's black minority it makes – from the most unlikely of sources – even better social sense.

PART 15

'Someone to Watch Over Me'

Keeping Ads Clean

It was one of the dilemmas of early television advertising that while commercials for laxative products had a comparatively free run, the word 'lavatory' could scarcely be uttered and it was forbidden to show the object itself on the television screen. It was all a 'question of taste' covered by the section 'Questions of Taste' in the *Notes of Guidance on Television Advertising* issued by the ITCA (Independent Television Companies Association) in 1964. The original *Principles for Television Advertising* was published in 1955 and superseded by the 1964 ITCA Code, but the section on 'taste' was virtually identical. The paragraph referring to the tasteless subject of lavatories stated unequivocally:

> TOILET CLEANSERS: Demonstrations of toilet cleansers must not show a shot of a lavatory pan, but a toilet cleanser may be shown on a bathroom window-ledge or being held above the actual toilet. This should not reveal any part of the toilet itself.

Since all the *Notes of Guidance* had statutory force, and so could not be regarded lightly, the advertisers of toilet cleansers had a hard time of it having to rely on the co-operation of the viewers' imagination to fill in the missing part.

For years, tons of Harpic, Sanilav and later Dot were consigned to an invisible destination in both animated and live-action films while the commentary told the story. Domestos was the first British product to enlist Orson Welles, as a voiceover – presumably an attempt to achieve maximum verbal impact. Brave Sanilav broke a verbal taboo in 1962 and earned itself a 'pat on the back for coming out with the word lavatory' from an anonymous writer in *Television Mail*.

As Independent Television approached the seventies, there was a slight concession allowing 'rim shots' that brought a vestige of reality to lavatory cleanser demonstrations, but it was not until 1971 that the pan-ban was lifted and the viewers were treated to a sight of *le tout ensemble*.

Opposite: While television advertising of foundation garments was tightly laced, popular daily newspapers were busting out all over. This full-page ad for the Playtex White Magic Living Girdle appeared in the *Daily Mail* in the summer of 1955. This advertising served the product well and nobody seemed to mind that the models were real and visible.

Toilet paper was another item in the ambit of 'Questions of Taste':

TOILET PAPER: Care should be taken when showing toilet rolls. They should not be shown installed and it is recommended that packshots should not be held in close-up for more than a few seconds.

Izal toilet paper tackled the problem in its early commercials by peopling the screen with cupids. The 'cupid ruse' was not uncommon with sensitive subjects, and was probably founded in some primitive belief that the gods of taste could be assuaged with a few chubby sacrifices.

Another nameless manufacturer found a different solution in 1962 that scorched its way into the psyche of the Earl of Arran – then a leading columnist of the London *Evening News* – compelling him to give a heavy pasting to the perpetrators. There was, he wrote:

. . . a dear pretty little girl building a castle out of toilet rolls. Higher and higher it mounts, then tumbles down – she starts again. I do not know who thought up this nasty idea, but he or she has nothing to be proud of. Nor has the ITA. If Sir Robert Fraser [Director-General, ITA] is really doing his duty keeping television advertisements clean he will have the advertisement withdrawn forthwith.

Lavatory paper advertisers kept trying. Children cut paper doll patterns from the stuff, and Andrex went so far as to coin a new word – 'stroft' (combining strong and soft) – in a linguistic attempt to communicate the message.

The former pioneers in this unenviable marketing scene – Izal, Jeyes, Velvet Jumbo (by Bronco) – eventually dropped out, leaving Andrex to stay the full course, albeit accompanied along the way by various soft newcomers.

Andrex seems to have cracked its presentation problem at last, using the well-tried formula of children and animals. In their commercials children watch with glee as a labrador puppy runs off trailing an unwinding roll of Andrex behind it, the first few sheets firmly stuck round its middle. This device enables both the length of the roll to be shown – in a final overhead shot – and its strength to be demonstrated. The locations are extraordinary – a small maze, a towpath, a shrubbery – always outdoor scenes. The juxtaposition of the paper with such tough natural obstacles gives it a strong image – so strong that it almost overstates the case.

Kleenex campaigned in the late seventies with a series shot much nearer to life, in urban surroundings. In the course of the films all sorts of people

ew! America's fabulous
fashion high-light for Summer

White Magic

Playtex LIVING GIRDLE
in white

It's like stepping into another world to see how this figure-flattering girdle slims and trims you from waist to hip to thigh. To feel the freedom that only the Playtex Living Girdle can give you. (That's why everywhere you go you hear about Playtex).

It's like no other girdle in the world — without a seam, stitch or

bone — invisible under the most clinging clothes.

Today, discover the beauty of White Magic. Thrill to the new wizardry of this fabulous American idea that slims you so naturally, so smoothly.

The only girdle that washes and dries in seconds and comes up glamorous, time after time.

At stores and good shops everywhere. Ask for 'WHITE MAGIC',
the white Playtex Living Girdle in the SLIM tube.

Sizes: For every age and figure. Also Petal Pink.

42/-

th comfort and complete freedom of action. Gives and breathes with you like
oth, seamless sheath right down to the suspenders.

© 1956 * TRADE MARK   PLAYTEX, 17 STRATTON STREET, LONDON, W.1
AND PLAYTEX PARK, PORT GLASGOW

In January 1960, just forty-eight hours before it was due to be screened, this commercial for Pex Pin-Pin nylon stockings was vetoed. Scottish Television insisted on it being withdrawn because the figures – known as the Pex Pixies – could have been mistaken for real naked models.

squeezed the Kleenex pack, emphasizing its softness. This was a step towards realism; people were seen to be handling the product, and this was the complete reverse of the Andrex whimsy. This approach has proved to have little impact.

One area formerly regarded as delicate has not only scaled the heights of respectability over the years but also – on one occasion – went over the top.

As a deodorant soap, Lifebuoy was in a far happier position than the products which came on the market with specific deodorant applications. Along with bodily hair removers, these too came under the dreaded 'Questions of Taste' ruling.

DEODORANTS AND DEPILATORIES: Demonstrations of the actual application of deodorants and depilatories should be avoided. Advertisements are more likely to be acceptable when emphasis is given to the good grooming and cleanliness achieved by their use. Impersonal or abstract techniques or presentations with an air of fantasy are preferable to direct illustration.

Animation seemed the only solution in the early days, along with a real packshot, Odo-ro-no and Sno-mist campaigned on television in the early sixties with animated films, but Bodymist in 1964 used quite an adventurous live-action piece of a woman with a towel draped round her. From the opening shot of bare feet and legs, the camera then rested on a view of her back with her arms slightly raised – the profile of her head in direct line with her armpit. This head to armpit shot became something of a cliché in deodorant commercials, and their progress was relatively untrammeled. The only time a deodorant product had a really bad press was in 1978 when a series of commercials for new 'Tickle' deodorant caused even the usually tolerant *Broadcast* magazine to comment, in supporting the called-for ban on the campaign, that it could not remember seeing such an overtly pornographic commercial.

It did seem surprising that the 'Tickle' commercials had survived the rigorous screening of the Copy Committee of the ITCA. The shape of the bottle with its roll-on top seemed to have come from a very blue blueprint. Added to this, the four young women on screen handled the bottle in a way that defied more innocent interpretation. The commercial was banned and has yet to reappear.

Depilatories never ran into such trouble, since ways of presenting them were limited to variations on hairless legs and armpits. This was not the case, however, with 'Foundation Garments', to which ITA attitudes were little short of puritanical. The 1964 guidelines for the advertising of foundation garments presented prospective advertisers with these conditions.

FOUNDATION GARMENTS: The use of a live model to illustrate the movements of a garment is permissible, provided the wearer is completely blacked out and shown against a black background. Close-ups of foundation garments worn by live models are not, however, to be allowed. In these cases dummies should be used. Any sales features which the advertiser wishes to emphasize should be portrayed diagrammatically.

There was a vast potential market for foundation garments in the late fifties and sixties which had hardly been tapped. The average woman spent £5 16s 1d per year on foundation garments in 1954. The television

One way to sell a
deodorant. Dress it up.

advertising history of Silhouette's foundation garments is a perfect
illustration of the rigours faced by the industry to meet these controls on the
display of their merchandise.

Given the launch in 1959 of its new U Bra, Silhouette opened on an
animated, twinkling U. From there to a close-up packshot, then a middle shot
of the pack moving on to several frames of the bra on a headless dummy. The
commercial ended with a shot of a shop display unit for U Bras, a close-up of a
real hand lifting a pack from the display, then two more packshots. With this
unexciting film the voiceover filled in the glamour.

'U'
'By Silhouette'
'The bra for you'
'A bra should hold you, mould you . . . but it should do more . . .'

'It should make you look more feminine, more vivacious . . .'
'More alluring so you are looked at, envied and admired.'
'All this, the U bra by Silhouette will do for you . . .'
'Try one on . . .'
'U, by Silhouette, gives you the look that *he* admires.'

A real-live woman wearing a bra in a revolutionary commercial.

Silhouette went on to launch the animated pixie that played a large part in its campaigns until the middle sixties, when it adopted a live model in an all-over black catsuit.

Berlei was similarly restrained in its commercials until the early seventies, when it appeared that the ITA might be about to lift some of the restrictions that had limited their advertising for so long.

In 1972 Berlei conducted a nationwide survey to see how women's shapes had changed since the 1920s – the last time they had surveyed the female population. This research was fortuitously timed, as the previous year the ITA announced an end to the ban on live models. The new-found freedom was used circumspectly at first but Berlei still met copy clearance problems on two occasions. The first when a woman, wearing a figure-hugging dress, smoothed it down the front in a completely natural way, and the second when a mother was seen wearing a bra in the company of her son of around two years of age. The complaint on this occasion was the use of a boy child in the company of a mother wearing a bra (and skirt). If the child had been a daughter there would have been no problem. The commercial was finally cleared without substituting the son when the advertising agency took a firm stand.

In 1976 foundation garments shook off the conservative image that had so stultified their television advertising when Berlei ran an excitingly shot commercial of a woman exercising in a studio. This was the beginning of the breakthrough to modernism and was followed a year later by its 'Secrets' campaign.

Triumph extended this approach a year later with its immensely cheeky, jump-cut, 'Triumph has the bra for the way you are' series. Oddly, after all the years of restriction on live models wearing underwear on camera, the general impression of both these campaigns was of the clothes the women wore.

But the biggest bra success of the late seventies, Gipsy by Berlei, was the one most at odds with the growing feminism of the time. It ran counter to fashion and almost everything else. Unashamedly male-oriented, the commercials have made Gipsy the strongest property in the bra market.

The first Gipsy commercials starred super-model Jerry Hall as a sensually tousled gipsy running through a large country house in the middle of a terrifying thunderstorm. There is a sense that she is being chased through the house – which was how the campaign was originally intended – with a hint of *droit du seigneur*. An original version showing a man following her did not please the ITCA Copy Committee.

Gipsy looks like being around for some time. Zetlands (the agency who created the campaign) prepared in late 1979 for the launch of Gipsy 2 in 1980. Casting sessions for the new 'Gipsy' girl were held during 1979 in New York, Paris, Munich, Los Angeles, London and Rome – a scale reminiscent of Otto Preminger's quest for an unknown to take the lead in his film *St Joan*, though far less publicized. 'Gipsy 2' was eventually discovered in Rome and may well set the trend for a succession of anonymous heroine figures – women of mystery – and start tipping the balance away from male domination of that role.

It is ironic that after only nine years of freedom to show foundation

The 'Secrets' were under their clothes.

garments on a living model, so reflecting the broadening attitudes of society today, the most successful bra commercial should have a seventeenth-century setting, when women tended to hold little social position.

The ultimate unmentionable was not even listed under 'Questions of Taste' but tucked away under a section on medicinal and semi-medicinal products, headed 'Feminine Hygiene, Feminine Disorders, etc.' In this context advertisers were told:

Owing to the possibility of causing offence or embarrassment to viewers, products offered particularly in relation to feminine hygiene and feminine disorders are unsuitable for television advertising, and the following points should be noted:
1. The advertising of products intended for the relief of menstrual pain, menopausal symptoms, etc., cannot be accepted.
2. Advertising for pads, tampons, etc., cannot be accepted.

Marie Helvin, the
beautiful gypsy.

3. Care must be taken to see that advertisements for analgesics, sedatives, health beverages and any other appropriate products cannot be construed either visually or verbally as offering the product for the treatment of feminine disorders.

4. References to the use of antiseptics and similar products for the purpose of feminine hygiene are not acceptable.

The blanket placing of these products under 'medicinal' demonstrated the desperate ignorance of those first arbiters of television advertising, to whom the subject must have proved the most embarrassing of all. Their misgivings seemed, none the less, to have proved valid. This area has had, understandably, no television advertising until the late seventies when a few manufacturers ventured into the medium. Their commercials have invariably drawn protesting letters to the IBA (ITA became IBA – Independent Broadcasting Authority – in 1972) – always from women who, in this, needed no pressure-group prompting. Space age mores are no match for primitive taboos.

PART 16
'You Ought to be in Pictures'

Animation in Commercials

Animation, which had been indispensable in advertising those products that so intimidated the ITA, was crucial to television commercials from the beginning. In the first few years of Independent Television nearly one-third of all commercials were animated.

The advantages of animation (including stop motion and photo animation) over live action (using real people and objects) were considerable, and not simply because cartoons were popular. Animation was able to transcend class, occupational and regional limits, of which agencies were so conscious in the early days. In addition it was of enormous practical help to agencies stricken by the prospect of creating TV campaigns with so little experience of the medium to go on.

Although probably unaware of it then, possibly even now, this country's television audiences have had the benefit of some of the world's finest animators through their work in commercials from 1955 till today. And for animators in turn, work in television commercials has led to their progress into the wider areas of film making.

Halas and Batchelor – John Halas and his wife, Joy Batchelor – was an established animation company in 1955. Their animated version of Orwell's *Animal Farm* had been universally acclaimed six months before the start of ITV, and they were in great demand for television commercial work. TVA, the film production company, obtained exclusive use of their services for two years from 1955 with a £75,000 contract. Three of their films appeared on the first night of ITV, advertising Guinness, Brown & Polson custard and Oxo cubes. Outstanding among their creations were the Murraymints characters, which were chosen by Alistair Cooke to be shown in America as representing British commercials at their most entertaining. The company is still as busy as ever.

Another animator with a first-night commercial to his credit is **Bob Godfrey**, who formed Biographic animation company with his partner Keith Lerner in 1954. Their first-nighter advertised Crompton Bulbs. Biographic launched

Above: The Murraymint
Guardsmen on parade
came from Halas and
Batchelor in 1955. The
horse could have stepped
right out of *Animal
Farm*.

Right: Joe, the 'Esso Blee
Dooler', was directed by
Nancy Hanna and Vera
Linnecar of Biographic
Cartoons.

Far Right: The 'Mother's
Pride' mother. TVC.

Maxwell House coffee when it was in small tins, and Godfrey produced the cartoons that accompanied the definitive jingle for *TV Times*. Animators generally work to the music track – and it was with these words in mind that the long-running campaign for the magazine was created:

Don't forget the TV Times,
Don't forget the TV Times,
The only way to see
What's coming on ITV
Is to go and get the TV Times.

In 1958, Godfrey went into live-action commercials for Courage beer. These were send-ups of silent screen melodrama, with old clips cut into the new footage to give a sense of authenticity. Godfrey played everything from wicked villain to brave rescuer, and the project gave full rein to the anarchic humour he had in common with Dick Lester and the Goons, with whom he had worked closely.

Best known of Biographic's characters was Joe, the tongue-tied Esso Blue paraffin salesman who called himself the 'Esso Blee Dooler'. Joe was created in 1958 when paraffin was a relatively common household fuel, but its use steadily declined over the years, as did Joe. Signor Buffo, the Esso petrol salesman whose voice was supplied by Dick Emery, was another long-lived Biographic creation.

George Dunning founded TVC (TV cartoons) in time for the advent of ITV, and the company produced some lasting characters. Most popular of all were Sammy and Susie Sunblest, the animated children in the Sunblest bread commercials. Voiceovers Denise Bryers (Sammy) and Maria Charles (Susie) completed the characters that saw Sunblest through its early television years. Sammy and Susie were so immensely popular that one Christmas they appeared on their own in a commercial to wish viewers a Merry Christmas. It was a commercial without precedent, as the product was not shown, but it was so effective that Sunblest's manufacturers, Allied Bakeries, were soon coping with stacks of Christmas cards addressed to Sammy and Susie.

TVC also created the Mother's Pride mother to launch Mother's Pride bread, product of a Manchester bakery. Thora Hird supplied the voice and the campaign succeeded in selling the loaf all over Britain.

A series of TVC films, using the tiny, Tam o'Shantered figure who still appears on the packs, introduced Golden Wonder crisps made by a small firm in Scotland. Until then Smiths were the only crisps on the British Market. Golden Wonder's success marked the beginning of a crisp Klondyke.

Mr Sheen, another TVC character, also remains on the product pack – an aerosol spray polish. He was voiced by William Rushton.

Richard Williams Animation was founded in 1955, but from then till its release in 1958 he worked mainly on his animated film *The Little Island*. His first commercial, 'Guinness at the Albert Hall', was shown in 1962 and collected several awards. More recently RWA animated the Cresta Bear, Tic Tac, the Brobat Loo Bloo and the blushing Johnson and Johnson baby. The Corona 'fizzical' orange was another Williams campaign.

The use of animation in commercials decreased in the early sixties as many talented live-action film directors began working on commercials and a new fashion was set. But from the ashes of that decline a group of bowler-hatted phoenixes arose to prove the exception. It took two Americans (Bob Geers and Bob Gross), a Londoner born of Italian parents (Tony Cattaneo) and an Englishman (Ron Wyatt) to home in on that most English stereotype – the city gent – and translate him into the most design-perfect animated character in commercial animation, the Spillers Flour Grader.

Homepride flour had previously advertised on television with live-action product demonstrations which showed little impact on sales. The Flour Graders, together with the matchless John le Mesurier voiceover, renewed the product's image, and sales took off. Geers-Gross formed their advertising agency on the Spillers' account and **Wyatt-Cattaneo Productions** was formed. Like other celebrated animated characters, the Flour Graders have always attracted fanmail. The ultimate tribute to their credibility was a request from the organizing committee of a Conservative party fête for a loan of their bowler hats.

Wyatt-Cattaneo went on to create the Dunlop Groundhog – the wild antithesis of neat Fred and his mates. The success of these and the Tetley Tea folk, Country Life buttermen, the Typhoo Gnu and KP crisp monks, and many other favourites, owes a great deal to the eye for detail in the animation precisely matching the ear for detail in the soundtrack.

Sammy and Susie Sunblest, brainchildren of Ronnie Kirkwood (now head of The Kirkwood Company). TVC.

The 'listening bank'
Gryphon, designed by
Ross Thomson and
animated by Richard
Williams Animation.

Midland

Come and talk to the listening bank

1968 was the great turning-point for animation with the release of *The Yellow Submarine* – the full-length animated feature film directed by TVC's George Dunning which combined the music of the Beatles with the dazzling graphics of Heinz Edelman. Dunning invested *Submarine* with a scale of ideas so innovative that they pushed back the boundaries of the art and brought animation to a new dawn. His influence was far reaching and a lasting memorial to the man. George Dunning died in March 1979.

Film titling and television commercials have much in common. Both are concerned with communicating essentials within a limited timespan. **Charlie Jenkins** had worked on *Yellow Submarine* and had also worked with Richard Williams on feature film title design. When he came to commercials in the early seventies it was with this background allied to his love for photography. In this context he had invented a projection system for photographs which enabled them to be screened with all the properties of film. This had, as well as fluidity, the added merit that the 'film' could be matched with music.

Jenkins' company, Trickfilm, has become identified with this technique – best illustrated in the Goggles sunglasses commercials and those for Listermint mouthwash. Trickfilm also made the extraordinary 'tapestry'

This Ben Truman ad was another product of Richard Williams Animation (1980).

films for Heinz. The effect of the tapestry completing itself is achieved by painting a complete tapestry, stitch by stitch, on a large piece of celluloid laid on top of a piece of canvas to provide the tapestry texture. The painting takes at least three weeks. The stitches are then gradually and literally wiped off and the artwork photographed at each stage. These photographs make up the finished film, which is run in reverse.

Oscar Grillo and Sergio Simonetti of Dragon Productions have contributed much to commercials of the seventies. Their work is typified by its sheer delight in characterization, and its quality rivals Disney's best output in the forties and that of Tex Avery of MGM and Warner Brothers. Briefed to animate a pilchard for Glenryck in 1977, they presented three films with the pilchard singing in the style of three well-known artists.

The Heineken commercial which had the three little pigs at the mercy of a much-refreshed Big Bad Wolf was an Oscar Grillo production. But Dragon's best-known work is probably the GPO's Buzby. Buzby highlights a rather disconcerting area of animated commercials. The first Buzby was animated at Richard Williams Animation and moved from there to a number of other companies. Although this shares out animation work, it also denies the kind of relationship between characters and animators which can be built on over a period of time. This passing-round of characters was unheard of in the early days of commercial animation.

Another more recent development concerns the degree to which the animator creates the characters for commercials – in which the animator used to play a positive part – working along with the advertising agencies to arrive at the right interpretation. Now animators usually work on characters that come to them as complete creations from the ad agency's art department.

Right: The very first Flour Graders (no arms showing), designed by Tony Cattaneo in 1965.

Below: Flour Graders (Mark 2), again by Cattaneo but more structured. After their first appearance it was soon obvious that they would be around for a very long time.

Above: Wyatt-Cattaneo also make Tetley Tea folk make teabags make tea sales.

Right: The Dunlop Groundhog (named 'Dumpy' in French commercials). Years before the Cresta bear he showed the effectiveness of line drawing. (Wyatt-Cattaneo).

Above: The animated Access card with the pound sign, who began as a walk-on character and now plays second lead. (Wyatt-Cattaneo).

Below: The Disneyesque finale of a Buzby commercial in which Spring came and melted the snowman.

This Lucozade commercial dramatically increased sales of the product within weeks of its first appearance. Drawn by Frank Langford from a live action film it was animated at Tony Cuthbert Cartoons.

A happy Awayday commercial for British Rail, animated at
Bill Melendez Productions in 1976.

The first Trickfilm Heinz 'Tapestry' commercial (1975). The original tapestry was worked by Nancy Fowler of Shirt Sleeve Studios.

Marie Helvin modelled the 'Goggles'. Husband David Bailey took the pictures and Charlie Jenkins directed this stunner in 1979.

Albert and Sidney, the Kennomeat dogs. Albert's voice started off with Peter Sellers; actor Leo McKern was one of several others who took over the Albert voice. Peter Hawkins provided Sidney's voice for the entire lifetime of the canine gourmets.

The animated willow pattern from the Knorr noodle tubs. Neat and witty animation, directed by Geoff Dunbar of Grand Slamm.

Tony Cuthbert, who also worked on *Yellow Submarine*, has enlisted the talents of press magazine cartoonists to design for commercials for Tony Cuthbert Cartoons. One recent campaign featuring the Inverbraw Grouse Beaters for McEwan's lager was designed by Bill Tidy. Cuthbert animated the Fox's Glacier Mint fox and bear. His most novel commercial proved a winner for Beecham's Lucozade in its first-ever animated campaign. It showed a woman walking along a graph signifying the ups and downs of her day. The animation merged into live action in the final frames.

Bill Melendez is a famous name in American animation, and his son, Steve, works in the London offshoot of his father's company, which has animated commercials for Abbey National, Boots and British Rail. Although a comparatively new animation company Bill Melendez was linked with one of the finest animators of the early television commercials – **Jacques Vausseur**, a Frenchman who came to work with Melendez when the company started eleven years ago. It was Vausseur who animated the earliest Babycham commercials, but his best-remembered work was on Kennomeat's Albert and Sidney.

Albert, the bullying dog, and Sidney, his meek master, were characters in a book called *The Dog's Handy Guide to Men* by adman Maurice Hitchings. He was invited to use some of the anecdotes from his book in order to warm up an audience waiting for a presentation of various ideas for campaigns to advertise a dogmeat product manufactured by a Scottish meat company.

Hitchings took the tension away from the affair with a couple of tales from his book, then the presentation got down to business. Afterwards, the Scottish client, accompanied by his son who had recently graduated from Harvard Business School, announced to everyone's astonishment (and prompted by his son's business instinct) that he wanted to feature the dogs in the company's commercials.

The campaign was animated by Jacques Vausseur and the voice of Albert was originally done by Peter Sellers.

In 1965, when Albert and Sidney were at the height of their fame, Jacques Vausseur flew over from Paris to London for a three-day visit. He forgot his passport and had trouble explaining to the customs officer who he was and the purpose of his visit. Finally he took paper and pencil and drew Albert and Sidney. The customs man smiled in recognition and allowed Vausseur to pass, after he had signed the sketch.

Grand Slamm is a relatively new animation company that has made a big impression in its few years of existence, and it was responsible for the animation in the Guinness commercial where the harp trademark began to

Guinness played on the harp strings and won the Kodak award for 'Craftsmanship in Commercials' (both animated and live action) in 1979. Directed by Grand Slamm's Geoff Dunbar.

play itself. Grand Slamm also animated the willow-pattern tubs for the Knorr noodles commercials.

The art of animation is going through a renaissance as far as television commercials are concerned, and the talent and skill is centred in this country. British animators are contributing commercials in even greater quantity for overseas. Twenty-five years of commercials have established an animation industry in Britain without equal in the world – and almost unrecognized in this country. It is probably about time our animators produced a commercial for themselves.

PART 17

'Try a Little Tenderness'

Voicing Over

Of all the skills that go into the making of a television commercial 'voicing-over' is probably the least recognized and most complex. It is also the loneliest.

No matter how much time has gone into the shooting of a commercial, the voiceover is generally added during the minimum half-hour session at the sound studio. At the beginning of the session the 'voice' sees the script, marks his/her sections and checks over with the agency representatives any particular points of delivery. There usually follow several screenings of the commercial which the voiceover watches from the tiny soundproof recording booth – the only link with the outside provided by earphones (cans).

All ideas that voicing-over can be done by anyone with a reasonable voice soon evaporate when 'Take 1' is called. At this moment the success of the whole campaign is concentrated on the perfect delivery of the message, not only vocally but in terms of pace and timing to fractions of a second. Since the average commercial is only 30 or 45 seconds long and the voiceover's contribution takes up only a part of this, there are no margins for error.

There are only about forty regular voiceovers working in television commercials today, and some of those have been in the business almost from the beginning. In the early years of Independent Television, voicing-over was regarded with some disdain by the acting profession, but this was as nothing to the contempt reserved for legitimate actors who appeared in commercials. While it was all very well for famous light entertainment personalities to be associated with TV advertising, there was what almost amounted to a blacklist operating among 'the profession' for those who dared to do the same, and they were often denied 'straight' work for years afterwards.

Frank Duncan, Richard Bebb and David de Keyser have provided voices for commercials for the best part of the lifetime of Independent Television. All were actors with experience of radio drama when they became involved with commercials, and none realized what an enormous business commercial television was going to become. All worked in the days of committee decisions on every little detail of a commercial and the client's presence

loomed largest of all. It was quite normal for the voiceover to turn up for the session and find between eight and twenty people waiting to hear the recording and then demanding endless retakes – over twenty being quite common – as if they all wanted to have a go at playing television directors.

Frank Duncan has always specialized in regional accents, and as a Scot he was the ideal voice for a big campaign for the Scottish *Sunday Express*. He did the voice with a strong but authentic Scottish accent, only to be told by the Scotsmen present – in broadest Glasgow – 'For Christ's sake, don't let everybody think we talk like this up there.' One of the most sensitive areas of revoicing is for the Irish market, where accents have sectarian connotations. The only solution is a non-existent 'Irish' acceptable to all.

In the days of live commercials the voiceover would sit by the mike ready for a cue that would simply consist of the words, 'Stand by, you're after the "so & so" ad.' This would be followed by several agonizing seconds watching the television monitor until the cue commercial faded signalling his turn to start.

Although there were relatively few 'voices' in commercials for the first five years, they were remarkably versatile. The David de Keyser who pitched the Tide message urging people to 'Get your clothes clean, not only clean but

A typical voiceover desk reveals that v/os are compulsive doodlers and exponents of graffiti. The booths are small and sparse, the walls baffled. Yet from this environment the voiceover communicates vocal magic.

'Old Spice, the mark of a man'. This voiceover is Steve Hudson, who won two major American awards against world-wide competition with his British commercial for *Sound International* magazine. The script demanded that he pronounce the magazine's title backwards.

deep down clean,' in one of the most strident and irritating detergent campaigns ever, was also the softly reassuring voice behind 'Headache? Tense nervous headache? Take Anadin.' De Keyser is also the man who reels off the long list of stores that follows the words 'Available at . . .' Quite simple for a man who can speak at the rate of 160 words per minute without faltering.

It did not, however, pay for a 'voice' to be too versatile, as actor Ron Moody learned to his cost in 1958 when, in December, the case of 'Sim *v.* HJ Heinz Co. Ltd and Another' went before Mr Justice McNair.

The 'Sim' was actor Alistair Sim, who had applied to the High court for an injunction preventing Heinz and their advertizing agents, Young and Rubicam, from continuing a particular television advertising campaign. The Heinz commercials were a series of cartoons bearing titles like 'Living like a Lord' and Ron Moody had supplied the voice for one of the figures – a voice which Alistair Sim took to be a perfect impersonation of his own. Friends of

Mr Sim also took the voice to be his and told him (he told the judge) that if he allowed his voice to be used in this way he was doing something beneath his dignity as an actor. Mr Sim had therefore decided, on the grounds that his voice – or what he was told was his voice – was being used, to start proceedings for libel, and for 'passing off'.

Mr Justice McNair did not feel able to rule on the question of 'passing off' being applicable to the unauthorized use of a man's voice whether he was an actor or not, although he granted it would be a grave defect in the law if it were possible for a person to make commercial gain by using the voice of someone else without his consent. The injunction was eventually refused, but the whole affair had a lasting effect on the world of voiceovers.

Actor John Carson has every reason to be conscious of the problem twenty-two years after that case. His voice has been mistaken for that of James Mason, to which it has a purely accidental similarity. He is sometimes asked to exaggerate that resemblance and 'do a James Mason' but has always

Left: The other 'man in black' – Bill Mitchell. Once he wrestled pumas, now he caresses words. Denim, after-shave, Seiko watches; as ursine as Welles. Just our Bill.

Right: Patrick Allen began the commercial voice revolution in the sixties. His voice was Canada dry and flinty. His delivery is compelling. As actor and voiceover Allen is a constant inspiration.

Miriam Margolyes, accomplished actress, versatile voiceover. Brooke Bond Dividend tea, Berger paint, Jif cream cleanser, HP beans . . . the list is endless.

refused. James Mason himself has never done an advertising voiceover.

Some years ago a relatively unknown voiceover did impersonate Mason's voice in a commercial for Vono beds, after which Mason's agent tried to bring an action against Carson – who had had nothing to do with it. The action was dropped. The final twist happened late in 1979 when he found his own voice being imitated by other voiceovers to the extent that listeners mistook the voicing style for his own. (One of Carson's best known copylines is 'Happiness is a cigar named Hamlet.') Carson can ill afford to be imitated so realistically. Over-exposure is one of the biggest enemies of the voiceover as it leads to devaluation.

Back in the day to day world of voiceovers the biggest problem was being a professional at the mercy of too many people who did not know what they were doing. Recording time was far more open-ended, and voicing sessions

dragged on with hair-splitting questions of tone and emphasis being discussed at disproportionate length.

It was American actor Hershel Bernardi, along with Daws Butler and Don Messick, who gave voiceovers their biggest break in this country. At the beginning of the sixties, copies of a recording called 'Blooper's Soap' (a blooper is an error or fluff) began to filter through to the British advertising business from the States. This was a send-up of a voiceover session in which the luckless v/o is forced to do one take after another in order to arrive at a version of the Blooper's Soap selling line that will please all the assembled admen. It was a brilliantly observed piece with the bite of authenticity that came from an inside knowledge of the business.

The recording not only highlighted exactly what British voiceovers were going through but also held up a mirror to some of the ridiculous posturing

Left: Marie Sutherland who voices for Fairy Snow, the Halifax Building Society, *Woman's Weekly* and many more.

Right: Joanna Palmer delivers the Persil Automatic message and voices for, amongst others, Playtex, Rennies, British Airways and Cookeen.

that was going on in the advertising business. Much of the American parody was the British reality.

Many brilliant people entered the television side of advertising and their influence is just as strong today, but others dazzled their way in, determined to get some of the glamour of television, and proved costly failures.

Sound engineer John Wood (now head of John Wood Studios) still remembers the day a new agency producer came to supervise a voiceover recording. The producer claimed to have vast experience, but on this occasion the agency boss briefed Wood beforehand to ask a couple of technical questions during the session, to test the extent of the new producer's knowledge. After a mind-bending thirty-seven takes the new man was finally satisfied, at which Wood asked if he needed any 'buzz track' (a technical term for atmospheric noise – a kind of natural recorded silence) at the end of the tape. The producer agreed to have some buzz track added. When asked how much, he said 1,000 ft would be enough (i.e. eleven and a half minutes), so earning his instant dismissal.

With the sixties came new voices and new styles of delivery, typified by the Patrick Allen more forceful, 'midatlantic' approach. Women were used far more than today, but because their vocal range is much wider a few women produced a great many female voices and one of the busiest was Valerie Singleton, later to spend so much time in front of the camera.

Actors began to lose their inhibitions about involvement with television commercials and audiences heard a far greater mix of voices, most of whom were not immediately identifiable with a famous face. By the mid-seventies the trend in voiceovers had shifted to voices which immediately called to mind well-known faces from television.

It was usual until the early seventies for actors to do voice-tests before being offered a particular commercial to do. Now the voice business is so streamlined – there has been a steady increase in 'voice agencies' in recent years – that testing is the exception and advertisers specify the voice by name.

Voiceovers have to be skilled in the art of post-synching i.e. synchronizing speech to film. This may have to be done for several reasons. First and rather sadly, some of the prettiest girls and most handsome men in commercials do not have a voice to match, or find it difficult to deliver a line at all. The client may just not like the original voice or may want a change of nuance which the original artist is unavailable to do. The commercial may also have to be post-synched if the original track has to be redone.

Many American commercials have to be dubbed with English voices – more difficult than dubbing a foreign language – and the most complex of those are those quaint ads for Grecian 2000 and Odor Eaters.

The attitude of the acting profession to voiceover work has completely reversed over twenty-five years. From being not quite the thing for any actor worthy of the name, it is now highly prized.

Voicing-over is the communicative art that demands most from an actor's inner resources in order to succeed, whether it is breathing life into an animated figure or outlining the merits of some branded product. The voice is capable of giving a renewed image or adding an extra dimension, as Tesco found out when they started the 'Checkout' campaign using a much softer vocal approach – untypical of their usual style. Actor Michael Jayston pitched the Tesco message as if to one woman. The tone invited but did not pressurize and the campaign was an outstanding success. Like most voiceovers, Jayston finds that definitions of his 'normal' voice vary immensely, so that he can be asked to do his 'normal romantic voice' or 'that cold, clipped, hard delivery, you know, the thing you usually do' and even 'that relaxed, man-next-door type. The kind of thing you do.' All of which demonstrates the extent to which voicing-over is acting.

Very few voiceovers have a wish to appear on-screen in commercials, although they are happy to be seen elsewhere on television. Like magicians with a precious illusion they want some of the mystery to remain.

Bruce Forsyth, one light entertainer who was always in demand for commercials, pictured in a 1959 TV ad for the *Daily Sketch* Pet's Police. The puppy took it seriously too.

PART 18

'Music, Music, Music'

Jingle Writers

Oh, the Brooke Bond van it's hurrying on its way
With a score or more deliveries for today,
Which means there's going to be
Fresh tea
For you and me,
As fresh as fresh can be,
It's Brooke Bond tea.

Dating from 1956 this jingle was sung to a tune reminiscent of 'The Deadwood Stage' from *Calamity Jane*. Its composer was Vivien Ellis – much better known for his musical comedies like *Bless the Bride*, with its eternal gift to soprano/tenor duos, 'This is My Lovely Day'. But it was BBC radio in the early fifties which provided the two greatest jingling talents in British TV commercials.

Cliff Adams and Johnny Johnson had almost parallel careers in BBC radio light entertainment. Both were composers and leaders of vocal groups, Johnny Johnson with the Keynotes and Cliff Adams with the Stargazers. Interestingly, the groups' names carried more than a hint of their leaders' styles and personalities. Johnson became the jingle writer with the common touch, while Adams' style is more reflective.

In 1954, Johnny Johnson was invited by an advertising agency to work on jingles for television commercials in the following year. This he agreed to do. Meanwhile, Cliff Adams' Stargazers were topping the charts with their second number 1 hit, 'I See the Moon' (the first, in 1953, was 'Broken Wings'). The record stayed at number 1 for fifteen weeks and was followed by several more hits.

At the end of August 1955, Adams received a phone call from an advertising agency asking whether he and his group would be interested in singing jingles for television commercials. Cliff Adams was really more interested in getting the Stargazers an appearance on Independent Television when it was underway, but decided to follow up the call and the Stargazers did record the jingle, which began with Dave Carey (one of the

Opposite: Chas & Dave, composers of 'Gertcha' ('Woooertcha' in their original version), also wrote the music for Butlin's 'Let's Go Butlin It' and the words for Rowntree's Breakaway jingle. Minstrels in the truest sense, writers for people.

group) yelling out, 'Hey that man there,' to which came the reply, 'Sorry, you'll have to wait – I'm finishing my Murraymint, the too good to hurry mint,' and then the jingle:

Murraymints, Murraymints,
The too good to hurry mints.
Why make haste
When you can taste
The hint of mint in Murraymints,
Murraymints, Murraymints,
The too good to hurry mints.

The jingle's lyrics were written by Harold 'Boogie' Barnes – one of the greatest influences on British television advertising – and the music was by Harold Fields and Joe Roncoroni. Cliff Adams was still unaware of the real significance of TV commercials. The Stargazers had released two more singles at the end of 1955 and these took up most of his time.

In March 1956 the Stargazers were invited to appear for a season at the London Palladium – the ultimate showbiz accolade. The Palladium bill included David Whitfield, Alma Cogan and Winifred Atwell, and Adams, realizing they would all be performing their 'latest hits', struck on an idea for the Stargazers' finale that would at least be different.

All went to plan, and after an introduction by one of the Stargazer girls that the group were going to present their latest recording, the orchestra struck up the introduction to the Murraymints jingle and the boys in the group returned wearing bearskins (like the guards in the commercial). They sang the jingle, then removed the bearskins, under which were concealed Murraymints that they threw into the audience.

The Palladium just fell apart at what was the undoubted sensation of the show, and it demonstrated to Cliff Adams a lot about the power of television commercials.

One of Johnny Johnson's earliest compositions was for a 'time spot' (i.e. an ad that lasted about 7 seconds) which achieved a special kind of celebrity. Over a visual of a 'smiling mug' were sung the words, 'Sleep sweeter, Bournvita,' followed by a yawn and the word 'Goodnight.'

Another early Johnny Johnson composition was for Rael Brook shirts. The circumstances of its composition reflect the breezy, spontaneous way decisions were made in the fifties.

Just three days before Christmas, Johnson was arranging to collect a surprise present (a Mini-Minor hidden half-way up the M1) for his wife and wondering how it could best be done when Harry Rael-Brook, shirt manufacturer, called at his home to tell Johnson he 'needed a jingle' as he had decided to advertise his 'Toplin' shirts on television.

Johnny Johnson sat down at the piano and asked Rael-Brook what kind of jingle he had in mind. 'Just something about Rael-Brook Toplin shirts you don't have to iron,' was the reply.

Almost in the spirit of calling his bluff, Johnson hammered out a few ascending chords on the piano and sang:

Rael-Brook Toplin, the shirts you don't iron,
Rael-Brook Toplin, the shirts you don't iron,
Rael-Brook Toplin, the shirts you don't iron,
Rael-Brook Toplin, the shirts you don't iron,

adding, 'Like this, you mean?'

Rael-Brook was delighted; and told the bewildered Johnson that the jingle was great, just what he needed. The Rael-Brook commercial went out with photo-animated shirts and the Johnson jingle and was an outstanding success, putting Rael-Brook Toplin shirts well and truly on the map.

Cliff Adams who, with Johnnie Johnson, has earned megajingler status.

Left: You and your car and Sealink. Rod Allen got them away a better way.

Cliff Adams composed and arranged the theme for Fry's Turkish Delight, and other memorable Cliff Adams jingles were for White Rain shampoo – 'There's a White Rain shampoo especially for you, White Rain, White Rain, White Rain' (like a Ziegfeld send-up); 'One man and his ale' – Watneys; 'Plump, tasty and delicious, The finest little fishes in the sea' – Skipper sardines; 'We're off to the land of wheat and honey' – Quaker Sugar Puffs; 'Hot chocolate, drinking chocolate – the late, late drink' and 'Cup hands, here comes Cadbury's' – both for Cadbury's Drinking Chocolate; 'When you've got Heinz spaghetti you've got taste on your plate'; 'This is you worthy Worthington' – Worthington beer; and many more.

Johnny Johnson was and is equally prolific. He composed the jingles that launched Maxwell House coffee; 'Now hands that do dishes can feel soft as your face' – Fairy Liquid; 'Softness is a thing called Comfort' – Comfort Fabric conditioner; and 'Mackeson, Mackeson, the world's a happier place, thanks to Mackeson.'

Johnson also composed the music for Shell petrol's campaign – 'Keep going well, keep going Shell.' He wrote the melody for the voice of singer Michael Holliday, who died soon after in tragic circumstances. Holliday's voice was nearest in timbre to Bing Crosby and it was Crosby who appeared in that first 'Keep going Shell' series. Sammy Davis also agreed to take part in the campaign. The Shell jingle has now been sung by more top singers worldwide than any other commercial jingle.

Johnny Johnson also composed what Cliff Adams calls 'the perfect singing jingle'. The words were by Mo Drake.

A million housewives every day
Pick up a tin of beans and say
Beanz Meanz Heinz.

The world of advertising has its Cole Porter in the person of Rod Allen, deputy chairman, creative director and founder partner of advertising agency Allen, Brady and Marsh. Allen is a musical wizard with a gift for communicating the essence of a product in words and music. In order to capture those qualities he pares down the product to its fundamental appeal and builds on that. The technique requires needle-sharp insight. For Woolworth he recalled childhood memories of the abundance of merchandise on display and arrived at 'The wonder of Woolworth's'. For Sealink, Allen listened to Sealink users who told him the real advantage of the system. This inspired, 'You and your car and Sealink. It's a better way to get away.'

One of his most popular compositions launched Berger's corporate campaign – an attempt to bring home to people the many kinds of paint the

A Monet-inspired Cadbury's Milk Flake commercial.

Joan Collins and Leonard Rossiter, directed by Alan Parker – perfectly paced comedy for Cinzano Rosé.

ABOVE: If René Magritte had imagined a TV commercial this could have been the one. The composition is infinitely interesting, and included on the set is a mock Magritte painting.

LEFT: A solitary record of the height of 'punk' from a 1979 Lee Cooper jeans commercial. The green eyes were achieved by coating contact lenses with a fluid which flared in ultra violet light. The punks were genuine, recruited through a newspaper ad.

Foster Grants, Foster Grants, frosty glance, Foster Grants. Fist of prince, flustered faints, lost gendarme, Foster Grants. Boss of France, imposter aunts, lotsa dents, twisty gents. Greased her palms, pots of plants, faster grunts, Foster Grants. Tasty tarts, takes a bath, sits on path, busts her front. Fussed we aren't, Foster Grants, forced a grin, Foster Grants.

. . . script for Foster Grant's 45-second commercial for Foster Grant sunglasses, 1979. Spectacular use of words and images.

Mothercare commercial, 1980. Positively integrated, uncompromisingly hopeful.

company produced. Sung by George Melly, it opened on a strong first line: 'Who makes the paint that's deep and sleek and gleaming on this Rover car?' This question format continues through the song with an answering 'Berger' until the name is firmly established. The last four lines tie it up:

> Berger, Berger,
> Ain't it quaint
> Nobody wants to know your name
> But everybody loves your paint.

For Wrigley's: 'Call it Wrigley's, call it spearmint, call it gum' and Toblerone (written with Harry Wander): 'Toblerone, out on its own, With triangular honey from triangular bees.'

A joint effort by Rod Allen and Johnny Johnson produced the all-time classic paean of praise to a carpet manufacturer:

> This is luxury you can afford,
> By Cyril Lord.

Another classic Allen/Johnson jingle was for 1,001 carpet cleaner:

> 1,001,
> 1,001,
> Will throw off that workaday frown.
> 1,001 cleans a big, big carpet
> For less than half a crown.

And to informalize the Midland Bank, Allen devised a piece vastly different to the 'part of the winning team' jingle which used to accompany its commercials. Now it's:

> Come and talk, talk to the Midland,
> Come and talk to the listening bank.

Cliff Adams and Johnny Johnson are exponents of a craft of jingle writing which uses music to serve the product to its best advantage. Jingles are a commissioned part of a total production, and an appreciation of this requires the professional approach that has kept them at the top for twenty-five years. Rod Allen is in this same tradition – but is a wordsmith as well.

In 1969 an entirely new approach to music in commercials was begun by Air-Edel – a company headed by composer/arranger/record producer George

Rael Brook Toplin – the
shirts you didn't iron.

Martin (whose work made such a contribution to the success of the Beatles)
and New Yorker Herman Edel.

Air-Edel's declared intent was to put music with commercials with the
emphasis on music – thereby changing the quality of advertising. There is a
kind of evangelism about the Air-Edel ideal which was expressed by
spokeswoman Maggie Douglas in 1979: 'I love music more than I love
advertising and want to give people the best possible music I can.'

The company has under contract some of the country's top composers and
songwriters. For example, Mike Batt, writer of acres of Womble music, was
the composer of 'Watch out, there's a Humphrey about' and the more recent
Smarties jingles. Perhaps the ace in Air-Edel's pack is Roger Greenaway –
winner of five gold and fourteen silver discs for songs he had co-written with
Roger Cook.

Before he joined Air-Edel, Greenaway had written 'The Real Thing' and
later, 'I'd Like to Teach the World to Sing' for Coca-Cola. Since signing up
with the company, Greenaway has jingled for Jacob's Club – 'If you want a
lot of chocolate on your biscuit join our club'; Richard Shops – 'are full of all
the pretty things'; Top Deck shandy – 'Top Deck, great taste'; and the song
which was performed by Rita Moreno in the commercial, 'If you feel like
feeling happy, pop a Pomagne.' Greenaway also co-wrote 'Jeans On' for
Brutus jeans, which became a number 1 hit.

One of the most imaginative musical castings for a commercial was the use of rockney (cockney rock) singers Chas and Dave in the Courage Best Bitter commercial set in an East London pub. The song they sang, 'Gertcha', had been part of their act for almost five years when they were asked to sing it in the commercial – with new lyrics. Soon after the campaign was launched, the single was released and became a big hit in the charts.

As well as revitalizing Chas and Dave's career the song brought a new dimension to music with commercials. For the first time, a piece of uncompromisingly regional (East London) music was used within an authentic setting and proved to be popular all over the country, which finally gave the lie to the doctrine of playing safe by using settings with which the maximum audience can identify. The record business realised some time ago that regional music had a national audience, and Chas and Dave have proved that it is not essential for TV commercials to address a mass market in mass terms.

Ronnie Bond is another prolific seventies jingler, composer of 'Only the crumbliest, flakiest chocolate, Tastes like chocolate never tasted before' for Cadbury's Milk Flake; and 'Switch to Michelin'. It was Bond's music, arranged for flute and clarinet, which backed the animated Lucozade commercials. He also brought punk to jingles for the first time with his music for the Lee Cooper jeans commercials. But his most unusual jingle contribution was the setting to music of the words on the Foster Grant's sunglasses commercial.

Jeff Wayne Music is the biggest company in the jingle world. It was founded by record producer Jeff Wayne to handle his own compositions. Wayne began composing jingles in 1970. It is his composition that heralds Esso's loping tiger and British Airways' 'We'll take more care of you'. Wayne also wrote 'The Abbey Habit' for the Abbey National Building Society. Wayne has a resident team of composers who have notched up a number of memorable jingles, including the piece that accompanies the Listermint 'Sloosh'.

In twenty-five years jingles have generally become much more structured and elaborate, although the old singable jingle tradition has not been lost. When Independent Television returned to the air after the long dispute which ended in October 1979, it did so with a jingle, 'Welcome home to ITV'. Oddly enough, it was composed by Cliff Adams, the same man who had been called on to provide music for the very first days of the service, twenty-five years ago.

PART 19
'Call Me No. 1'
The Record-Breaking Ansafone

One of the eternal questions about television commercials is the one about whether or not people pay attention to them and hence whether they work at all.

Apart from the endless surveying that goes into collecting evidence about the effectiveness of commercials, there is more tangible proof that audiences respond – in the shape of the largest single number-answering service in the world, which is situated at Thames Television's building in London's Euston Road. The installation was an indirect result of the disappearance of 'admags' when television companies had to devise a format for holiday advertising that would allow holiday operators to get their information over to the public.

The solution was found in the introduction of 'themed breaks' – a commercial break given over to one kind of advertising – at the end of which viewers were told that further information was available by writing to the holiday firms or by filling in the coupon in *TV Times*.

In 1969, as an experiment to tie in with campaigns for winter holidays, Thames Television decided to install thirty-six telephone-answering machines at their London headquarters and publish a telephone number with the holiday commercials. The London area, having the highest rate of telephone installations – 25% of the viewing area – was an ideal place to begin. The thirty-six lines proved quite inadequate for the demand, and by 1970 the number of lines was increased to eighty. By the end of the year the number of lines totalled a hundred. The answering service began to be used by other advertisers – mail-order companies etc. who would previously have relied on people filling in coupons for information.

London Weekend Television, seeing the success of the Thames venture, decided to operate its own answering service, and for several years the two companies ran with their separate telephone numbers. This meant that commercials in the London area had to be made with two different endings – one for weekdays on Thames and the other for weekends on LWT. Finally, the two companies joined to form the 'London Television Answering Service' – a seven-day-a-week operation.

When viewers call the published number they are linked to the answering tape and asked what information they require – and their request is recorded. For the last seven years the voice on the answering tape has been male, which cuts down appreciably on the number of nuisance calls the previous female voices attracted. It is quite common for the machine to cope with 15,000 calls in one evening in the London area alone. Other television companies have adopted similar services for their own areas.

The next step in dealing with viewers inquiries involves a roomful of transcribers, who work through all the message tapes, directing requests to the appropriate advertisers. It is at this stage that the nuisance calls become evident, but all have to be heard through to the end in case a genuine inquiry is missed. Sometimes these calls add a bit of spice to the work of transcribing, and there is occasional entertainment when a caller treats the answering service as a kind of television audition by singing or reciting poetry . . .

The London Television Answering Service operations room with its banks of cassette machines.

Inset: Unmasked – for London area TV commercial viewers who have rung the familiar information number. Stuart Fenwick is the man behind the voice which asks what information is required and instructs callers on the message machine.

PART 20
'Thanks for the Memory'
Winning Some, Losing Some

It is still said, by critics of television commercials, that people will buy anything which is advertised on television. While it may be true that people will buy anything that is advertised on television *once*, there is abundant evidence that they exercise the right not to buy again. Here are a few of the products which didn't quite make it:

WIRL – Washing powder launched in 1960.

LUXURLOAF – Sliced white bread, wrapped, containing 10 thick slices and 15 thin. (1963)

WALPAMUR FLY-KILLING PAINT (1965)

WALL'S CORNETTO – 'A little piece of Italy for only a shilling' – flopped in 1965 but returned in the seventies as

> 'Just one Cornetto,
> Give it to me,
> Delicious ice-cream
> From Italy'

. . . and never looked back.

DOVE – 'And down came Dove' toilet soap. And out it went quite soon. (1965)

DUO-CAN – A meal in a can, open one end to find rice, open other end to find meat. Pour meat on top of rice. (Too few people did.)

LYRIL – 'Get that lovely lively Lyril feeling' toilet soap. (Not enough people wanted the feeling.)

DIAL – Soap detergent.

Leslie Mitchell presented this commercial for a 'piece of machinery' (purchase price £10,000) in 1959. Two genuine inquiries resulted from the ad. An object lesson for media buyers. Television has proved to be most successful for 'shopping basket' items. But, nothing ventured . . .

PART 21

'Well, Did You Ever'

Tiny Tales

* In October 1959 the managing director of Sutherland's Paste withdrew £4,600 pounds worth of advertising from Granada Television because the company did not play the National Anthem at the end of the evening's transmissions.

* In 1967 when French actor/comedian Fernandel was dropped from the Dubonnet commercials in which he had appeared since the campaign began – 'Do 'ave a Dubonnet' was his slogan – it was revealed by the advertising agents that 'he doesn't speak a word of English. He could not even say "Do 'ave a Dubonnet".'

* Jim Henson's Muppets appeared in American television commercials before most of this country knew what a commercial was.

* In February 1960 the General Municipal Workers Union advertised itself on television.

* It was announced in 1963 that Her Majesty's Navy would no longer be available to appear in commercials for Senior Service cigarettes – thus breaking eight years of Navy co-operation with Senior Service advertising.

* In 1963 a critic called Coca-Cola, 'presumably the drink for confused, with it, young people'.

* A six-minute commercial for the Vauxhall Viva was shown in 1963.

* In April 1965, Jimmy Durante appeared in a commercial for Kellogg's cornflakes, This was what he said: 'Extracrispyactivatedappetiza-lisherated corn.'

* When ITV opened, Sir John Barbirolli, conductor of the Hallé Orchestra, announced that no programme in which he appeared with the Hallé would have commercial breaks.

* An early campaign for Flash cleanser was based on the copy line, 'Flash

cuts cleaning time in half.' One commercial was filmed at the London Palladium, where Flash was to be used to clean the stage. To add authenticity the director decided to have three acrobats on stage and sent someone to find three men to fill the bill. The men were found at a circus, and when asked to pose, each on the other's shoulders, the director was surprised to find that the man on top needed a ladder in order to get into position, and began to get worried when he immediately fell off, hitting the stage like a sack of coal. The scene was eventually completed after six takes, in which the luckless man at the top plummeted to the stage every time.

It was only later the director learned that the three were not acrobats but lion tamers who had heard the adman at the circus ask if anyone wanted to earn £25 for a day's work, and did not want to pass up the chance.

* In a commercial shoot on a river another director was anxious to include some ducks that were swimming nearby, but they kept swimming just out of shot at the vital moment. The problem was solved by attaching a piece of string to each duck's leg and tying a brick to the other end, a perfect anchor.

Seeing a better location further up river, the crew moved the ducks to the new stretch of water. Unfortunately it was deeper than at the original spot and the ducks immediately sank with the weight of the bricks. The tale had a happy ending as the crew dived in and brought every duck to safety.

* TV comedy actor Chris Emmett went to discuss his part in a commercial with the director and clients. Knowing only that he was to play the part of a prison warder, Emmett listened as his role was detailed until it came to the piece of the action where he was to reach into his pocket for a bar of chocolate and eat a piece. There was an embarrassed silence as Emmett explained that chocolate made him sick. The director took this to mean 'fed up' with chocolate, at which Emmett had to explain, more graphically, that he had an allergy to chocolate and one bite would make him physically ill. The director even asked him if he could possibly manage to eat one piece and then be ill off camera, but there was no way round it and the representatives of the chocolate company were left chastened to have met someone who couldn't eat their product without suffering.

The Top Twenty TV Commercials for the four weeks from 12 December 1979 to 8 January 1980 (compiled by TABS)

 1. Fiat Strada
 2. Don't Drink and Drive (COI)
 3. Texaco
 4. Smarties
 5. Parker Pens (Alfred Marks)
 6. Cinzano Rose (Leonard Rossiter and Joan Collins)
 6. Coca-Cola
 6. Milk
 9. English Cheese
 9. Quality Street
11. Heinz Soups
11. Black & Decker Workmate
11. PG Tips Chimps
14. National Dairy Council Cream
14. Harvey's Bristol Cream Sherry
16. Woolworth (Harry Secombe)
16. Sekonda (Ronnie Barker)
16. Milk
16. Dunlop Tyres
16. Hamlet Cigars ('Christopher Columbus')

PART 22

'As Time Goes By'
Statistical Swings and Roundabouts

The last twenty-five years have seen a major shift in the British lifestyle. Independent Television, the only medium capable of communicating an advertising message simultaneously to an entire population, has existed for all of that time. The key question, and possibly one which can never be answered, is whether a link can be found between this kind of mass advertising and social attitudes. Whether, if the ITA Act had failed in Parliament and the BBC had been granted non-commercial second and third channels, British society would have undergone the same changes.

Media Expenditure Analysis Ltd (MEAL) has produced figures on every area of advertising expenditure since 1967. Before this, similar but not compatible figures were listed in Legion Publishing's *Statistical Review*. The figures reveal that certain products which were advertised consistently in the early years of ITV have vanished from the TV screen, while others never, or scarcely ever, advertised have shown an increase in advertising expenditure that far exceeds the expected average.

One small but telling example of a disappearing product is starch, which was a regular TV advertiser until 1966 when it ceased to feature in commercials. The reasons for its disappearance could concern the use of shirt collar stiffeners or even the adopting of more casual wear. People had become less 'starchy' by 1966, the age of 'England swings'. It could have been just coincidence that a product with such connotations of propriety bowed out at that very time, but perhaps a glance at another rather ordinary household item will shed more light.

Shoe polish advertising has dwindled steadily since 1972, the beginning of the inflationary spiral. Well-polished shoes used to be the sign of a 'gentleman', but less attention is perhaps paid nowadays to this tradition. The introduction of synthetic shoe materials has also cut down on the need for old-style polish.

Home-perm advertising left the TV screen in 1964. This was the time when long straight hair was fashionable and, in itself, an escape from the look-alike waves of the perm. Uniformity of hairstyling was giving way to individual self-expression. Personality hairstylists began to emerge – most

First shown in 1978 to advertise Campari. Directed by Brian Byfield it starred Robert Saachi and Lorraine Chase. As time went by 'Casablanca' returned and rekindled the Bogart magic.

memorably Vidal Sassoon – who set the countrywide pattern which shattered the 'shampoo and set' establishments and launched tens of thousands of 'cut and blow dry' parlours.

Starch, shoe polish and home perms are all external indicators, but the decline in another once mighty product category points to a different kind of change.

The 1955–1978 TV advertising expenditure figures for laxative advertising show astonishing peaks, far above the average. In 1958 a staggering £303,000 was spent advertising laxative products on television; the expenditure on bread and bakeries for the same year was around £179,000. 1962 was a similarly big spending year, with expenditure of £305,000, (average yearly figures between 1955 and 1966 for laxative products were between £150,000 and £250,000). The 1964 figure leapt to £343,000 and in 1965 it was £356,000. The all-time high was reached in 1969 with a total of £597,000, then the decline began, ending in 1978 with a trifling annual expenditure of £37,000.

There seems to be no easy explanation for this odd set of figures, but one

possible reason could be that people have become less preoccupied with 'inner cleanliness', as Andrews liver salts used to call it, and more interested in the world outside themselves.

This trend towards wider horizons is illustrated in figures for airlines, which spent a minimal amount on television in the first ten years, the main advertised services being small internal flights. When Pan-Am began advertising transatlantic flights in 1965, one adman commenting on the first commercial wrote, 'Surely a very small proportion of the British television audience is ever likely to fly to America.' And yet from 1969 when the spending was £783,000 – reaching £1,168,000 the following year – the annual total has dramatically increased (nearly £4m in 1978).

National tourist offices – the 'Come to Spain/Malta/Morocco/Singapore, etc.,' type of advertising spent a mere £17,000 in 1969. The figure increased rapidly to £69,000 in 1970, and by 1978 had reached £1,228,000.

Leisure items too have shown a steep rise in expenditure on television, with photography-related goods showing the first significant boom in 1970 when £533,000 was spent. By 1978 this stood at £3,537,000.

Luton Airport was the gateway to fame and fortune for Lorraine Chase.

The two-minute commercial for Fiat Strada cars, first shown in June 1979. Directed by Hugh Hudson and shot to a specially arranged version of Rossini's *Barber of Seville*, it was sung by Niall Murray. It was universally acclaimed by the 'professionals' and voted No. 1 ad in the Dec. '79/Jan. '80 TABS (Television Advertising Bureau (Surveys) Ltd) poll.

Below: Retail store advertising is another major growth area on television. MFI furniture stores use the medium heavily. This production still illustrates the streamlining and convenience afforded by video rather than conventional filming. The 'set' is an actual MFI store. Not too long ago 'video' was regarded as a callow upstart medium, but by the end of 1980 video commercials are predicted to outnumber filmed ads by 20 per cent.

Opposite: Two commercials – twenty years apart. The black and white was directed by Kenneth Hume for Arrow shirts; the colour ad was made in 1979 for Lee Cooper jeans. In both, youth challenges the camera and, through it, the viewer. Both feature vertical lines. The mood is the same: Take note, we are here.

Sue Bryan, the 'nice face' who was with the 'nice place' – Woolwich Equitable Building Society.

More remarkable still has been the growth in advertising records, cartridges and cassettes – a mere £3,000 for the whole of 1970 but by 1978 this had soared to £12,682,000.

Motor car manufacturers used to place very little reliance on television advertising, with a few exceptions – the launch of the Triumph Herald (showing the car drive down the steps of the Albert Hall), the introduction of the Issigonis Mini and other such special occasions. The pattern changed significantly in 1973 with an increase of just under £1m from the previous year's figure – from £761,000 to £1,677,000. After a minimal drop in 1974, spending increased from £5,098,000 in 1975 to £12,810,000 in 1978. This kind of advertising budget must be seen as worthwhile investment by the motor trade and illustrates, despite the energy crisis, the expanding market for cars.

At times of economic crisis, expenditure on luxury items would be expected to drop in favour of staple products, but the trend in advertising of luxuries is upward in every sector of that market – sherry, vermouth and mixer drinks expenditure has climbed steadily upward over the last ten years, along with toilet waters and perfumes, while flour and baking powder, key thrift indicators, showed a reduction in advertising in 1974 and have fluctuated, with a downward tendency, ever since.

Perhaps the biggest character change in advertising spending has been in the financial advertising of building societies and banks, with credit card promotion only just beginning to dip a toe in the lake of possibility.

rolling home!

All makes of old records are urgently needed for salvage to maintain the already limited production of new records. Please sort out all you can spare and take them to any record dealer, who will buy them from you irrespective of whether you purchase any new records.

Decca

records...radio...television

So much depends on
INNER CLEANLINESS

The human machine is every bit as responsive to internal cleansing as a motor car is. How can it be expected to work all the while impurities remain? Neglected poisons get into the bloodstream and cause headaches, digestive upsets, dull eyes and spotty skin.

Deep down Inner Cleanliness gives you the finest foundation for fitness. And how simple it is to achieve! Just a glass of tonic, refreshing Andrews whenever the system needs its cleansing aid. Try it and see how much fitter and brighter you feel.

FIRST .. Andrews cleans and refreshes the mouth and tongue.

NEXT .. Andrews settles the stomach and corrects acidity, the chief cause of indigestion.

THEN .. Andrews tones up the liver and checks biliousness.

FINALLY .. To complete your Inner Cleanliness Andrews gently clears the bowels. It sweeps away trouble - making poisons, relieves Constipation, and purifies the blood.

ANDREWS

Tonic · Refreshing · Health-giving

Family size tin 2/-

Guaranteed to contain 8 ozs.

(44-3)

That "GOOD–morning" Feeling!

Out of bed bright and early—singing in the bath —breakfast!—*then* what? It all depends on the breakfast. The system properly nourished with WELGAR SHREDDED WHEAT, the digestive organs not over-taxed, and that cheery *good* morning feeling is still there to carry you through and keep you smiling. If you live in one of our permitted areas, get some to-day, and make sure that every morning is a *good* morning. 8d. per large packet (3 points).

WELGAR SHREDDED WHEAT
REGISTERED TRADE MARK
Made by The Shredded Wheat Co., Ltd., WELwyn GARden City, Herts.

Above left: Ten years before ITV's first night the newspapers told a different story, as this Decca ad shows.

Above: A mid-Forties newspaper ad stressing the importance of 'regularity'.

Shredded Wheat's mid-Forties press advertising highlighted selling points which disappeared when it went on to television (three points referred to 'Ration Books'). Stressful times they were and digestive organs were cherished.

Two kinds of nostalgia, fifteen years apart – a commercial for Dunlop children's shoes directed by Kenneth Hume, and the classic Hovis 'Bike Ride' commercial directed by Ridley Scott in 1974.

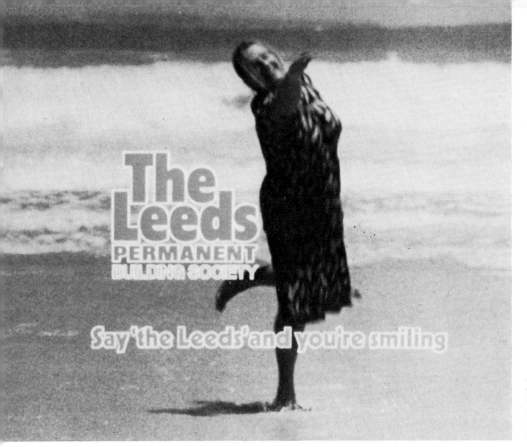

What is beauty? 'Say the Leeds and you're smiling' proved in this Fellini-esque shot that beauty is exuberance and humanity regardless of the female shape. The great Federico watched a reel of British TV commercials at a private showing in London fifteen years ago and said at the time, 'How can these people produce such little masterpieces lasting one minute?' The maestro would surely approve of the spirit of this finely composed shot.

Joan Collins and Leonard Rossiter, directed by Alan Parker – perfectly paced comedy for Cinzano Rosé.

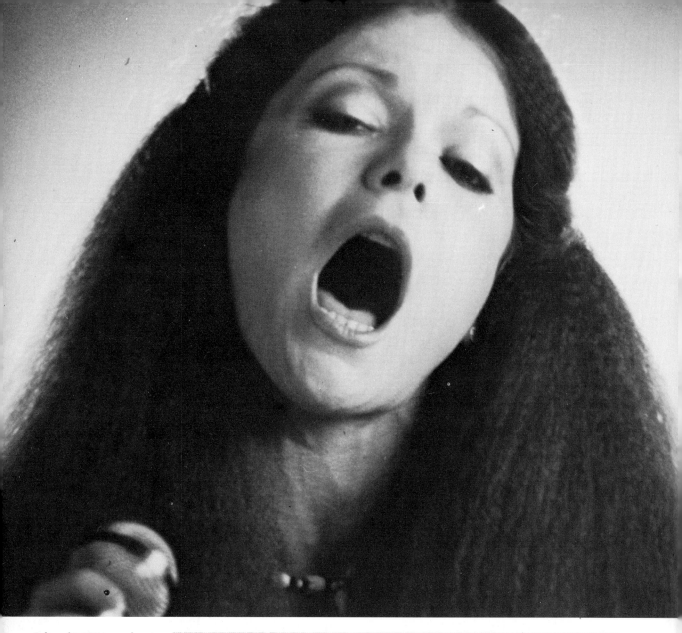

Sales of BASF tapes leapt 62 per cent as a result of this commercial starring singer Jenny Haan. The director was Peter Webb.

The image of children has changed dramatically in the last twenty years. Although the same toys have play appeal this 1959 admag shot is curiously restrained and studious.

The most surprising major investor in TV commercials has been the Government's Central Office of Information (COI), which in 1975 – the year marking the beginning of the energy crisis – was the biggest spender of all.

Road safety, fire and crime prevention, and TV licence evasion have all been the subject of COI commercials, as well as those campaigns showing the dangers of drinking and driving and not wearing seat belts. But COI commercials are not simply about informing the public. They are, less obviously, about saving money by cutting down on the economic consequences of accidents in terms of police and emergency services, hospital and other medical care, working days lost and all the other demands on resources that accidents create. The COI is also responsible for services' recruitment.

The highs and lows of TV advertising expenditure over the last twenty-five years of TV commercials will almost certainly redistribute themselves over the next quarter of a century. There were already small indications of change at the beginning of 1980 when a home perm was advertised on television for the first time in sixteen years. Unheard-of products are bound to emerge while currently familiar ones will disappear.

As for the 'tuppenny Punch and Judy show', after twenty-five years its real identity must be obvious. It will remain what, in fact, it always was. The most expensive roller-coaster of them all.

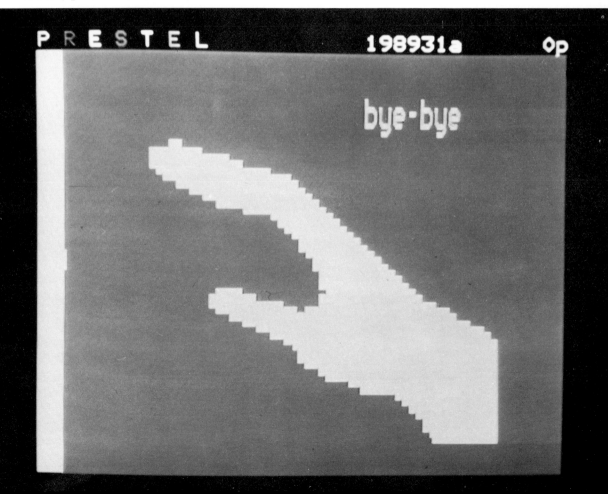

Acknowledgements

The illustrations in this book are reproduced by kind permission of the following (numbers refer to page numbers):

Cliff Adams: 167 (*above*); *Advertisers Weekly*: 15, 16, 17, 18, 19, 20, 21, 26–30, 51, 52, 121, 133; Patrick Allen: 159 (*right*); Associated-Rediffusion: 37, 61 (*above*), 75, 77, 78, 79; BASF-Zetland's: 188 (*above*); BBC Copyright: 6, 8, 9; Beecham's-Foote Cone & Belding Ltd: 104–5; Beecham's – J. Walter Thompson: 42, 120; S. H. Benson: 97; Berlei-Zetland's: 137, 139, 140; Biographic: 142 (*below left*); Birdseye – Collett, Dickenson, Pearce & Partners Ltd: 70, 71, 72; Birdseye – Lintas: 69; Brooke Bond Oxo Ltd – Davidson, Pearce, Berry & Spottiswoode Ltd: 84–9; Brooke Bond Oxo Ltd – J. Walter Thompson: 110–13; Cadbury Ltd – Foote Cone & Belding Ltd: 98; Cadbury Ltd – Leo Burnet: 106–7; Cadbury/Typhoo – Boase Massimi Pollitt Univas Partnership: 92, 93, 94 (*below*); Cinéaste Assoc: 153 (*above*); *Commercial Television News*: 35, 109; Lee Cooper – Zetland's: 183 (*below*); Tony Cuthbert Cartoons: 150; *Daily Mail*: 39 (*above*); *Daily Mirror*: 39 (*below*); *Daily Sketch*: 44 (*right*), 55; Dragon Productions: 149; Simon Drew: 160, 161; Ray Elton: 25, 127; *Evening Standard*: 185 (*below*); Fiat – Collett, Dickenson, Pearce & Partners Ltd: 182 (*above*); Findlater Mackie Todd & Co. Ltd – J. Walter Thompson: 180, 181; *Flight International*: 22; Elida Gibbs – J. Walter Thompson: 123; Grand Slamm: 153 (*below*), 155; Guinness/Harp – Charles Barker City: 99 (*below*); Halas & Batchelor: 142 (*above*); Halford's – Boase Massimi Pollitt Univas Partnership: 129; Steve Hudson: 158; IBA: 31; Leeds Permanent Building Society – David Williams & Ketchum: 187 (*above*); Lever Brothers – J. Walter Thompson: 57 (*below*), 62, 63; Bill Melendez Productions: 151; MFI: 182 (*below*); Midland Bank – Allen, Brady & Marsh Ltd: 128; Nevs: 101, 102; Nicholas Parsons: 94 (*above*); Rank Hovis Macdougall – Collett, Dickenson, Pearce & Partners Ltd: 186 (*below*); Geo. G. Sandeman & Sons Ltd – Pritchard Wood Partners: 99 (*above*); Sealink – Allen, Brady & Marsh Ltd: 167 (*below*); Valerie Singleton: 80; *Sunday Chronicle*: 44 (*left*), 185 (*above*); *Television Mail*: 33, 46, 47, 49, 57 (*above*), 59, 61 (*below*), 65, 73, 81, 115, 117, 134, 136, 163, 170, 175, 183 (*above*), 186 (*above*), 187 (*below*), 188 (*below*); Thames TV: 173; Tower Bell: 165; Trickfilm: 152; TVC: 142 (*below right*), 144; Voice Over Ltd: 159 (*left*); Richard Williams Animation: 145, 146; Woolwich Equitable Building Society – Ogilvy Benson & Mather Ltd: 184; Wyatt-Cattaneo: 148

The author would also like to thank Rod Allen, publisher of *Broadcast*, and Bernard Barnett, editor of *Campaign*, for permission to reproduce material from *Television Mail* and *Advertisers Weekly* respectively.

Thanks also to the undermentioned for their time, help and reminiscences.

Cliff Adams
Rod Allen (ABM)
Brad Ashton
David Barker
Jeremy Beadle
Brian Beagan
Richard Bebb
Tony Bilbow
Brian Bishop
Martin Boase
Terence Brook
Denise Bryer
Jeff Burton
Tom Bussman
John Carson
Tony Cattaneo
Joy Clark
Graham Clutterbuck
John Coates
Norman Collins
Dennis Conway
Tony Cuthbert
Barry Davies
David de Keyser
Colin Doeg
Maggie Douglas
Mo Drake
Simon Drew

Frank Duncan
Ray Elton
Nick Evans
Keith Ewart
Mike Fensome
Stuart Fenwick
Malcolm Fishwick
Winston Fletcher
Ian Fordyce
Norma Fryer (IPA)
Vic Gardiner
James Garrett
Joe Garwood
Neville Gates
Fiona George
Colin Gibson
Bob Godfrey
Carl Gover
Chris Greening
Oscar Grillo
John Halas
Peter Hawkins
Patrick Hayes
Chas Hodges
Peter Hoyes (TABS)
Steve Hudson
Michael Jayston
Charlie Jenkins

Johnny Johnson (jingler)
Johnny Johnson
Ronnie Kirkwood
Roger Lambert
Keith Lerner
John May
Barry McDonald (IBA)
Nicolette McKenzie
Steve Melendez
John Miell
Bill Mitchell
Jim Norton
Mike O'Donovan
Julie Orchard
Rosie Oxley
Brian Palmer
Nicholas Parsons
Dave Peacock
Gordon Phillips
Philip Purser
Peter Richardson (BBRK)
Stuart Ruttlidge (ITCA)
John Schlesinger
Stefan Sergeant
Chris Sharples
Tom Sheridan
Lloyd Shirley
Sergio Simonetti

Valerie Singleton
Chris Smith
Jack Smith (IBA)
Neville Smith
Tony Solomon
Lorraine Southin
Reg Starkie
John Stockley (MEAL)
Sue Stoessl
James Strettell
Cathy Stringer
Berny Stringle
Denise Sweny
Harry Theobalds (IBA)
Owen Thetford
Dennis Vance
John Webster
Fay Weldon
Ron Wiles
John Wilkinson
Rex Williams
John Wood
Tom Wright

Thanks finally to Alan Samson at Michael Joseph

Index